ROAD BIKING ™

Washington, D.C.

Help Us Keep This Guide Up to Date

Every effort has been made by the authors and editors to make this guide as accurate and useful as possible. However, many things can change after a guide is published—trails are rerouted, regulations change, techniques evolve, facilities come under new management, etc.

We would love to hear from you concerning your experiences with this guide and how you think it could be improved and kept up to date. While we may not be able to respond to all comments and suggestions, we'll take them to heart and we'll also make certain to share them with the authors. Please send your comments and suggestions to the following address:

The Globe Pequot Press
Reader Response/Editorial Department
P.O. Box 480
Guilford, CT 06437

Or you may e-mail us at:

editorial@globe-pequot.com

Thanks for your input, and happy travels!

ROAD BIKING™

Washington, D.C.

Michael Leccese and Rolf Pemberton

FALCON®

GUILFORD, CONNECTICUT
HELENA, MONTANA
AN IMPRINT OF THE GLOBE PEQUOT PRESS

_A_FALCON GUIDE®

Photo credits: pages x, 6: Bill Clark, courtesy of National Park Service; page xv: Fred Fizell, courtesy of D.C. Development Land Agency/National Park Service; pages 3, 16, 41, 49, 57, 62, 105, 176, : Rolf Pemberton; pages 11, 34, 46, 100, 122, 147, 156, 170, 187: courtesy of Edward M. Reardon; page 27: Jack Rottier, courtesy National Park Service; pages 28, 124: courtesy of Historic American Buildings Survey; pages 48, 68: courtesy National Park Service; page 81: courtesy Montgomery County Historical Society; page 86: courtesy of United States National Arboretum; page 93: Paul Thomas; page 106: Paul Souders, _The Montgomery Journal_; page 142: M. Woodbridge Williams, courtesy of National Park Service; page 165: Cecil W. Stoughton, courtesy National Park Service.

Text design by Leslie Weissman-Cook
Maps by Trailhead Graphics © The Globe Pequot Press

Library of Congress Cataloging-in-Publication Data
Leccese, Michael.
    Road biking Washington, D.C. / Michael Leccese [sic] and Rolf
    Pemberton.—1st ed.
        p.   cm. — (Road biking series) (A Falcon guide)
    Includes bibliographical references.
    ISBN 0-7627-2305-X
        1. Bicycle touring—Washington Metropolitan Area—Guidebooks.
    2. Washington Metropolitan Area—Guidebooks. I. Pemberton, Rolf.
    II. Title. III. Series. IV. Series: A Falcon guide

GV1045.5. W18L425 2003
917.5304'42—dc21   2002044700

Manufactured in the United States of America
First Edition/Second Printing

To Kathryn,
for everything

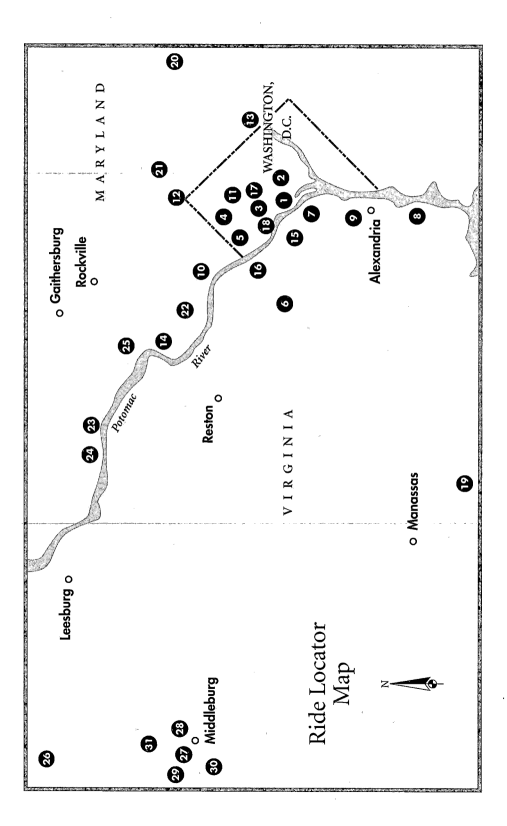

Ride Locator Map

Contents

Appendix

Preface

The rides chosen for this book bring to it the flavor of the Washington, D.C., area. Rides were chosen due to their proximity to parking or Metrorail stations. Enjoyable routes carefully balance traffic, historic highlights, scenery, and, of course, safety.

The research for this book rests on a wealth of information from visitor centers, cycling groups, local cyclists, and other authors. Many thanks go to all those who contributed time or information. I am especially grateful to Jeff Serena, David Singleton, and the rest of the gang at The Globe Pequot Press for their support in this project. They are really and truly a pleasure to work with. Last but not least, the book could not possibly have been completed without the support of my ever-understanding wife, Kathryn, and the company of my riding buddy and good friend "Duo Flats" Dylan.

Introduction

Washington, D.C., and environs are an urban cyclist's dream. The metropolitan area of three million people finds room for 48,080 acres of parkland and more than 670 miles of paved, off-road multiuse trails. The city and its suburbs have also designated 480 miles of signed on-road bike routes. And if weather turns foul, cyclists can jump on Metrorail, the region's 70-mile subway system.

Starting from the city's social and historic center, Georgetown, you could ride to Mount Vernon (16 miles); the foothills of the Blue Ridge Mountains (60 miles); Cumberland, Maryland (180 miles); or the Oz-like Mormon Temple (10 miles)—while encountering hardly a single automobile. Staying within city boundaries, you could visit the Lincoln Memorial, White House, Smithsonian museums, and U.S. Capitol, all within one hour of easy pedaling.

Not surprising for a city of political activists, Washington boasts the nation's largest regional bicycle club, the Potomac Pedalers Touring Club (PPTC), and its own two-wheel transportation lobby, the Washington Area Bicyclists Association (WABA). In 1988 *Bicycling* magazine named D.C. one of the top ten U.S. cities for cyclists. In 1998 the League of American Bicyclists (LAB) moved their national headquarters to Washington, D.C., where they have better access to policy makers affecting cyclists in America. First formed in 1880 as the League of American Wheelmen, LAB promotes bicycling for recreation and transportation.

In *Captive Capital* (Indiana University Press, 1974) Sam Smith describes Washington as ". . . one of the most attractive, civil, interesting and pleasant [cities] in the country." Geography is part of what makes it so. Washington is located at the confluence of two rivers, where the coastal plain collides with the Piedmont foothills. Near the city line, the Potomac rushes over Class VI ("risk-of-life") rapids to meet estuary waters lapping up from the Chesapeake Bay. The old Federal City sits low on former swampland; the newer outskirts rise as high as 400 feet on bluffs overlooking the Potomac.

If Washington seems an anomaly among U.S. cities, perhaps it is because it is a planned city, founded by congressional fiat in 1790 and laid out by the brilliant, stormy French engineer, Pierre Charles L'Enfant. L'Enfant based his baroque street plan on elements of eighteenth-century London, Paris, and Rome. Much of his vision survives: the broad avenues cutting diagonally across a grid of streets, the stunning vistas of monuments, and the abundant groves of trees.

L'Enfant conceived a diamond-shaped city 10 miles square, divided into four quadrants: Northwest, Southwest, Northeast, and Southeast. This can cause confusion. There is both a 1000 Pennsylvania Avenue N.W. and a 1000 Pennsylvania Avenue S.E.; there are two A Streets with near-identical addresses, four First Streets, and so on. In 1846 Arlington County and Alexandria reverted to the Commonwealth of Virginia, leaving the Potomac River as a natural boundary for the Northwest and Southwest quadrants.

Predating the founding of Washington were the eighteenth-century ports of Georgetown and Alexandria. Today these national historic districts are the focus of tourism. Both feature cobblestone alleys, colonial houses, cozy narrow streets, and excellent access by bicycle. You can still find one of the city's original boundary markers on Alexandria's edge.

Since 1966 the metropolitan area has been shaped by a new boundary that has effectively extended the city limits: the Beltway, a 66-mile superhighway looping around Washington. The Beltway can be a cyclist's bane, since it blocks many pedaling routes out of the city. This book will attempt to be your passkey through its concrete fortifications.

Freeways aside, D.C. has some of the nation's strictest zoning and planning laws. As a result of a 1910 law, no building may rise higher than twelve stories, or about 130 feet. Development near parks and public buildings is subject to review by the Fine Arts Commission. Here you find an asset rarely visible in Manhattan or even Pittsburgh: the horizon.

Culture in all its forms enlivens life in the nation's capital. Easily accessible by bicycle are all the monuments, more than 150 embassies, the Kennedy Center, 70 museums, colonial historic districts, and restaurants ranging from Afghani to Vietnamese. Because the city population is nearly 70 percent African American, it is also home to an African-American university, several museums of African-American history and art, and landmarks such as Cedar Hill, the former residence of abolitionist Frederick Douglass, now owned and interpreted by the National Park Service. Moreover, there are Hispanic neighborhoods in Mount Pleasant and Adams-Morgan, a Vietnamese section in Arlington, and a vestigial Italian area downtown.

In Washington life has improved for local cyclists. For example, the National Park Service spent $1.5 million on an elevated path near Theodore Roosevelt Island, thus connecting two routes and creating one of the nation's longest contiguous bikeways. The 64-mile path connects Mount Vernon with the Blue Ridge foothills to the west.

Today cycling in the Washington area seems poised for a breakthrough. Fed up with traffic and pollution, regional governments are weighing a $60 million plan to connect regional trails and lanes into a 1,000-mile system complete with standardized signs—a sort of interstate system for bicyclists.

This ambitious plan recognizes that a bicycle is an environmental tool. I hope readers will use this book not only for pleasure rides but also to plot rides to work, to run errands, and to visit friends and family. In some small way, you'll directly prevent pollution and ease the demand for more highways and parking lots. And yes, you'll save lots of money, too—fewer repair bills, insurance premiums, or payments for a second car.

That said, this region could be far more hospitable to bikers. There have been setbacks: D.C. eliminated the position of bicycle coordinator from their city government. And the suburbs continue to sprawl with relatively little regard for either bicyclists or pedestrians.

I urge readers of this guide to become advocates of bicycle transportation. Join the Washington Area Bicyclists Association and the League of American Bicyclists. Lobby your workplace to install a shower and safe bicycle parking. (Many offices already have a shower, installed long ago by some jogging executive. Ask your office manager to remove the old files so that you can reclaim the space.)

Be sure that your local, county, and state representatives know you support bicycling. Find out what trails are being planned and state your support for them. Here are two for starters: the Metropolitan Branch from Union Station to Silver Spring and the continuation of Capital Crescent from Silver Spring to Bethesda (the paved segment from Bethesda to Georgetown was completed in 1995; hard-packed gravel trails still remain between Bethesda and Silver Spring). Build those two, and Washington will have a Bicycle Beltway.

CLOTHING AND GEAR

For comfort and ease of operation in the Washington, D.C., area, there are a couple of quick items to think about: the local weather and the route the ride takes. D.C. in the summer is hot and humid! Pack more water than you think you'll need—at least a bottle of water for every hour you plan to ride. Wear, and pack, sunblock—especially if you'll be riding around the middle of the day. Always take some extra money and some change in case you need to buy more water or equipment from locales detailed along the ride.

Consider cycling clothing that is light in nature and readily wicks sweat and moisture away from your body. Cycling shorts are one item that you will not want to do without. Above all else, ensure that your cycling clothing is comfortable and try not to "test out" new items on longer rides. Consider wearing padded cycling gloves; these buffer the vibration and road shock that can lead to numbness. Gloves will also help minimize injury should you fall.

For downtown riding, a bell is advisable if only to assist you with notifying pedestrians that you are approaching. Accompany the bell with a polite call to them in advance to advise them that you're passing (". . . on your left . . . thank you!").

If you think you will be riding before sunrise or after sunset, your bicycle must have proper lighting.

A WORD ON SAFETY

The biker looking to conquer the capital should take some precautions, such as the following:

1. *Wear a helmet.* Traffic here is insistent, swift, and sometimes abusive to cyclists.

2. *Buy the strongest U-shaped lock you can find.* Bicycles are more likely to be stolen than cars here. Be sure to secure both wheels and the frame to a fixture such as a bolt-down bike rack or a double parking meter. Better yet, bring the bike indoors or lock it in a parking garage if the bike rack is within sight of the attendants.

3. *Carry maps.* The bikeways have been improved, but the rivers, train tracks, and freeways form many obstacles and dead ends. The city's quadrant system can easily confuse newcomers. All too often meandering cyclists find themselves on four-lane roads or two-laners with blind curves and no shoulders. It isn't worth the risk, and there's usually a better way through. (The maps included in this book should help greatly. If you do veer off the routes, a good local map will help you get righted.)

Note: A symbol on the maps—R—indicates rest room locations.

4. *Realize that off-road multiuse trails aren't for bikes alone.* Despite common terminology, they are *not* exclusively "bike paths." Share them courteously with families, hikers, in-line skaters, and equestrians, as well as other cyclists.

5. *Take a buddy.* Washington's crime problems have been well publicized, and while I've never felt afraid, I would advise cyclists to ride in pairs and carry spare parts and tubes.

THE DIFFERENT KINDS OF RIDES

1. *Rambles.* Rambles are the easiest and shortest rides in the book, accessible to almost all riders, and should be easily completed in one day. They are less than 35 miles long and are generally on flat to slightly rolling terrain.

2. *Cruises.* Cruises are intermediate in difficulty and distance. They are generally 25 to 50 miles long and may include some moderate climbs. Cruises will generally be completed easily by an experienced rider in one day, but inexperienced or out-of-shape riders may want to take two days with an overnight stop.

3. *Challenges.* Challenges are difficult, designed especially for experienced riders in good condition. They are usually 40 to 60 miles long and may include some steep climbs. They should be a challenge even for fairly fit riders attempting to complete them in one day. Less experienced or fit riders should expect to take two days.

Arlington Memorial Bridge

ABOUT THE DIRECTIONS

All rides include step-by-step directions and maps. Starting points can be reached by auto or Metrorail and are often near bike-rental facilities. See the section about Taking Your Bike on Metrorail, below.

Some of the rides (23 and 24, for example) may be combined into longer routes. While some rides are planned as loops, others are one-way rides that require doubling back the way you came. In the latter cases I've tried to include optional side trips to historic or scenic sites that will vary the scenery on the return trip.

Rides 25 through 31 are longer and more challenging trips. Novice or out-of-shape cyclists should try the shorter rides first.

Local cycling clubs and regional park authorities can help plan rides. Most publish maps. Some even organize weekend rides. I've included a list of cycling sources at the back of this book.

TAKING YOUR BIKE ON METRORAIL

Many of these rides can begin at Metrorail stations, which is especially helpful for those living in the city without owning a car. The Metrorail should be applauded for its recent effort to embrace cyclists. It has completed a study in reducing the hassles for cyclists choosing to use Metrorail to supplement their riding.

Still, you can't simply board the train anywhere and ride to your destination. You *can* now take your bike on the trains without a Metrorail Bike-on-Rail permit so long as you observe the rules. Ideally, ask the station manager upon arrival for details concerning rules governing taking your bike on the Metrorail. The station managers are extremely helpful and sincerely caring. They keep an up-to-date copy of the rules in brochures that they can provide you with.

Bicycles are permitted on Metrorail (limited to two bicycles per car) weekdays except 7:00 to 10:00 A.M. and 4:00 to 7:00 P.M. Bicycles are permitted all day Saturday and Sunday as well as most holidays (limited to four bicycles per car). Bicycles are not permitted on Metrorail on July 4 and other special events or holidays when large crowds use the system.

The significant rules currently in place are that you:
♦ Enter and exit through the first and last—not the center emergency—doors. In an emergency, place your bicycle on the seats and leave it on the train.
♦ Only regular bicycles are permitted (maximum size 80 inches long, 48 inches high, and 22 inches side). No tricycles or training wheels are allowed.
♦ Use the elevator at all times. Do not take bicycles on escalators. Avoid blocking doorways and aisles. Yield to other passengers.

♦ Do not ride bicycles in stations or on platforms or trains. Keep both wheels on the ground and the kickstand up. Maintain control of your bicycle.

♦ If you are under sixteen years of age, you must be accompanied by an adult.

Please observe these rules and recognize that breaking the rules could not only get you suspended from using the Metrorail services, but also impact whether others are allowed to continue using the Metrorail services.

For the latest information about taking your bicycle on Metrorail, contact Metrorail at (202) 962–1051 or visit their Web site at www.wmata.com/metro rail/bikeonrails.htm.

OFF-ROAD CYCLING

If you bought a bike in recent years, chances are it was an all-terrain or mountain bike. For routes suitable for all-terrain bikes, see rides 11, 14, 19, and 23. When riding an ATB, take care not to trespass on hiking trails or disturb wildlife areas. We all need to do our part to prevent the National Park Service and other park authorities from having to ban knobby-tire bikes in many areas.

A WORD ON CLIMATE

Washington's summers can only be described as torrid. The typical August mercury hovers around 95 degrees, with comparable humidity. Moreover, the summer air quality can be atrocious. During many summer days, the pollution (most of it generated by the area's millions of cars) makes exercise unhealthful.

The region atones for the intolerable summer season with lingering warm autumns and springs and mild winters. To wit, I tested most of the rides included in this book during a particularly sunny January with temperatures of about 50 degrees.

You can beat the summer heat by rising early to complete short rides before 9:00 A.M. You'll find that Metrorail also comes in handy. When the sun drops and the wind rises at about 6:00 P.M., I like to take off for Mount Vernon, timing the trip so that I arrive at Alexandria's King Street station at about sunset. The air-conditioned ride home is particularly refreshing.

HOW TO USE THIS BOOK

This book contains scenic rides throughout the Washington, D.C., area. Each ride profile includes photos, a detailed map, and includes information that will help you choose a ride that matches your fitness level and interests.

Ride summary: Provides an at-a-glance paragraph of the ride highlights.

Start: Where the ride begins.

Distance: The ride in miles.

Approximate pedaling time: A range of time in hours it will take the average cyclist to complete the route and to stop at points of interest.

Terrain and surface: Lists the topography and the type of roads (major highways, rural roads, and so forth) and road surfaces (rough, potholes, gravel/dirt).

Things to see: Points of interest along the route.

Traffic and hazards: Lists road hazards you should be aware of, including high traffic volume, presence or absence of road shoulders, presence of railroad crossings, and warnings for rough road surfaces.

Facilities: Lists the types and location of rest rooms, restaurants, and shops on the route.

Options: Lists other routes or tours accessible from the ride.

Getting there: Detailed directions to the start of the ride.

Ride description: Detailed description of the ride, which may include information about attractions, history, geology, and wildlife.

Miles and Directions: Lists the turn-for-turn mileage directions for the ride as well as additional options for exploring. It is highly recommended you ride with a cyclometer so you can use the mileage points for each profile.

Local information: Lists local chamber of commerce offices, visitor centers, and other agencies that can provide you with information about the ride.

Local events/attractions: Lists fun events and attractions you may want to visit before, during, or after your ride.

Accommodations: Lists recommended bed-and-breakfast inns, hotels, hostels, and other accommodations available on the ride. The hotel and bed-and-breakfast finding services listed are recommended by chambers of commerce in Washington, D.C., Virginia, and Maryland. These services provide a wide range of accommodation needs.

Bike shops: Lists bike shops that are located in close proximity to the ride.

Maps: Lists other map sources for reference.

Monuments on the
Waterfront Ramble

This route combines human-made marvels with the natural beauty of the Potomac River and, for those fortunate enough to ride it in early April, the heralded Tidal Basin cherry blossoms that draw residents and tourists alike. This 13-mile loop incorporates stretches of the D.C. and Virginia banks of the Potomac and views of the Pentagon, Lincoln Memorial, and Seward Johnson's massive statue The Awakening. The terrain is mostly flat, except for Arlington Cemetery, making it suitable for novice cyclists. The ride could take weeks if you savored all the riches en route. This is Washington at its most Athenian.

Start at the Harry T. Thompson Boat Center, where you can rent boats and bikes (March to November). If you are arriving by car and parking here, be aware of the three-hour limit in this metered lot. Head southeast on a bikeway that runs past the Watergate Apartments and between the Kennedy Center and the Potomac River. Built in 1970 on the site of the Heurich Brewery, the 630-foot-long performing arts center contains the American Film Institute movie theater, an opera house, a stage for major plays, a concert hall, a cabaret, and restaurants.

After riding past volleyball courts and through two narrow bridge underpasses (dismounting recommended), you will arrive in 1.3 miles within view of the Lincoln Memorial, at the John Ericsson Monument at Independence Avenue and Ohio Drive S.W. Carved from granite and dedicated in 1926, the Ericsson statue pays tribute to the designer of the U.S.S. *Monitor*, the ironclad warship that fought the Confederate ironclad *Merrimac* during the Civil War.

View the Lincoln Memorial in profile and proceed downriver on Ohio Drive, with the polo fields of West Potomac Park on your left and the Tidal Basin beyond. (Time your ride for a summer Sunday afternoon if you want to watch part of a polo match.)

Washington's newest monument, the Franklin Delano Roosevelt Memorial, is along this stretch of Ohio Drive. Opened in 1997, it joins the memorials to Washington, Jefferson, and Lincoln as major tributes to four great American leaders. Rather than a grand marble structure, the Roosevelt Memorial consists mainly of a series of contemplative outdoor gardens.

Approximately 0.8 mile ahead lies a brief but graceful bridge stamped 1909 and ornamented with gargoyle fountains. Cross it and turn right at the circular flower bed to stay on Ohio Drive. Pass under four bridges for automobiles, Amtrak, and Metrorail, and then begin a 3-mile, one-way loop around East Potomac Park, a popular picnic area that features an Olympic-size pool, a golf course, and many flowering trees.

At the park's apogee is Hains Point, fronting the confluence of the Potomac and Anacostia Rivers and Washington Channel, a waterway full of pleasure boats. Across the channel lies old Fort McNair and its impressive brick buildings. The tall, domed edifice is the Army War College, founded by Theodore Roosevelt after the Spanish-American War. Reagan National Airport is directly over the Potomac.

Hains Point beckons when you see huge fingers and a large bearded head rising from the ground. The startling figure is Seward Johnson's 1980 statue *The*

Awakening, which portrays a Brobdingnagian figure rising from the soil. Have your photo taken perched on one of the large aluminum digits, then proceed upstream, parallel to the Potomac River.

Return via the loop to the 1909 bridge. Instead of crossing, turn right toward the Jefferson Memorial. Built in 1943, this domed pavilion ringed by fifty-four columns houses a 19-foot-tall bronze statue of Thomas Jefferson and inscriptions of his words. The memorial fronts the Tidal Basin and its famous crescent of cherry trees, whose early-April blooms are cause for citywide celebration.

Returning to the parking-lot entrance, look for a curb cut leading to a bike path over the Fourteenth Street (George Mason Memorial) Bridge. The bikeway over the span is an engineering marvel—wide, smooth, and well protected from the main roadway. You'll have views of the Pentagon, sailboats, and bridges carrying Metrorail and freight trains over the river. At the base of the bridge on the Virginia side, bear right onto the Mount Vernon Trail, which parallels the George Washington Memorial Parkway. Take an immediate left to begin your return upriver.

With the Potomac on your right and Boundary Channel on your left, pedal 0.25 mile and over a little bridge to the graceful Navy and Marine Memorial, dedicated to Americans lost at sea. Ride a few hundred feet more to the southern edge of Lady Bird Johnson Park. Designated in 1968 to honor the arboreal-minded first lady, the island park is planted with 2,700 dogwoods and 1 million daffodils (carefully counted, according to the National Park Service). Just over the parkway (a dicey crossing for cyclists) stands Columbia Island Marina and the fifteen-acre Lyndon Baines Johnson Memorial Grove, planted with hundreds of white pine trees surrounding a memorial stone shaped from pink Texas granite. Continue on the trail toward Arlington Memorial Bridge, dedicated in 1932 to symbolize the reunion of North and South. Bear left on the trail to avoid passing under the bridge, and ford two striped crosswalks across the George Washington Memorial Parkway. Cross a traffic circle to reach Memorial Drive, gateway to Arlington National Cemetery.

Ride on the sidewalk to avoid the macadam road surface. Pause to ponder *The Hiker*, a 1965 statue dedicated to veterans of the Spanish-

Pausing across the water from the monuments

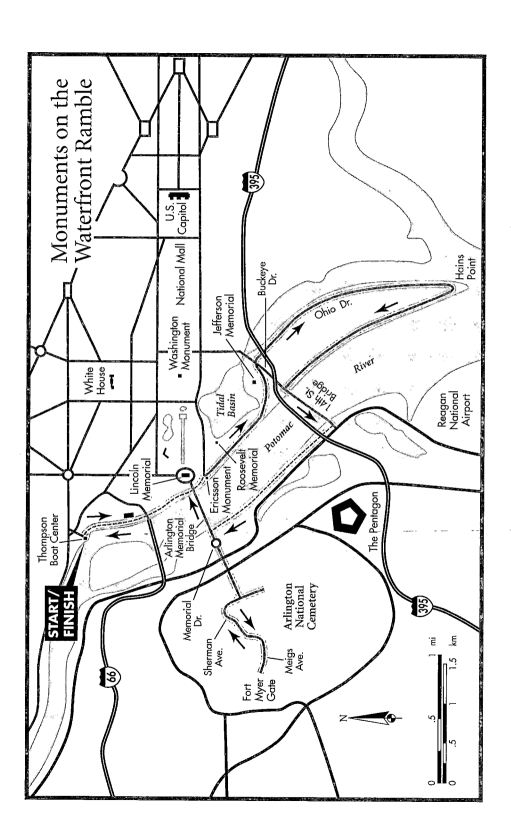

Monuments on the Waterfront Ramble

START/FINISH

White House

U.S. Capitol

National Mall

Washington Monument

Lincoln Memorial

Thompson Boat Center

Arlington Memorial Bridge

Ericsson Monument

Roosevelt Memorial

Tidal Basin

Jefferson Memorial

Buckeye Dr.

395

Ohio Dr.

Hains Point

14th St. Bridge

Potomac

River

Reagan National Airport

The Pentagon

395

Memorial Dr.

Sherman Ave.

Arlington National Cemetery

Meigs Ave.

Fort Myer Gate

66

N

0   .5   1 mi
0   .5   1   1.5 km

Note: Use blocks and features to navigate instead of miles.

◆ From Thompson Boat Center, right on trail heading toward Watergate Apartments and Kennedy Center, Potomac River on right.

◆ Cross parkway intersection to reach path. Continue between outdoor volleyball courts.

◆ Ride (or dismount and walk) through two short bridge underpasses. Bear right with bike path onto Ohio Drive at Ericsson Monument.

◆ Proceed southeast for 0.8 mile on Ohio Drive past Roosevelt Memorial on left. Cross 1909 bridge. Turn right and follow signs to East Potomac Park (Hains Point).

◆ Cross under four bridges. Left at stop sign onto Buckeye Drive to begin loop of East Potomac Park.

◆ Right at stop sign onto Ohio Drive.

◆ At end of one-way loop, keep straight on Ohio Drive. Pass under four bridges. Do not cross 1909 bridge. Bear right toward Jefferson Memorial.

◆ Across from parking-lot entrance to memorial, access Fourteenth Street Bridge bike path via curb cut on right.

◆ Cross bridge and bear right on bike path. Turn left at T.

◆ Proceed upriver on Mount Vernon Trail past Navy and Marine Memorial and Lady Bird Johnson Park.

◆ To reach Arlington Cemetery, bear left at fork in trail and cross George Washington Parkway three times at crosswalks marked with stripes.

◆ At Memorial Drive, stay on sidewalk. Detour to visitor center on left.

◆ At end of Memorial Drive, turn right onto Schley Avenue. Continue uphill via Sherman and Meigs Avenues to Fort Myer gates. Turn around and return to Memorial Drive.

◆ Using Arlington Memorial Bridge sidewalk, cross to D.C. to Lincoln Memorial.

◆ Take unmarked road back to Ericsson Monument.

◆ Retrace path back to Thompson's.

American War of 1898. Across the road is the Seabees Memorial; note their proud "Can Do" motto. The cemetery's visitor center is on the left, halfway down Memorial Drive. Lock your bike to one of the iron gates (no bike racks) if you want to go inside for information.

At the massive stone gate marking the end of Memorial Drive, turn right onto Schley Avenue to make a short tour of the grounds. The route is well marked, as are roads off-limits to bikes. Continue up Schley to Meigs Avenue, which leads to the Lee Mansion (Arlington House) high on a precipice with a view of the river and the monuments of Washington. This is a good place to park and explore the cemetery on foot. On the way back, visit a marker honoring city planner Pierre L'Enfant. This spot offers a magnificent view of down-

The Jefferson Memorial

town Washington. Then retrace your ride to the Memorial Bridge.

♦ Gingerly cross the traffic circle again to reach the bridge's sidewalk, which you can ride back to Washington. Pass by the two enormous, golden equestrian statues symbolizing Valor and Sacrifice, and bear right at the end of the sidewalk. Again, carefully make your way across the traffic circle (preferably on foot) to the Lincoln Memorial grounds.

♦ Built in 1922 to honor the author of the Emancipation Proclamation, the memorial has since been a magnet for civil rights activism. Here, in 1939, black singer Marian Anderson performed her famous concert, defiant of segregation, and in 1963 Martin Luther King uttered his "I Have a Dream" speech to a throng of 200,000. Architect Henry Bacon designed the building in the style of a Greek temple with Roman detailing. Sculptor Daniel Chester French created the 900-ton figure of Lincoln from twenty-eight blocks of white Georgia marble. Beneath the memorial lies a catacomb created by the construction. It's actually filled with stalactites and stalagmites formed by water dripping from the marble steps.

Flanking the Lincoln Memorial, and directly across from the Vietnam Veterans Memorial, is the site of the Korean War Veterans Memorial, a monumental landscape that features life-size-plus statues of soldiers marching across a reflecting pool. The memorial was dedicated in 1995.

Now you can either return to Thompson's or pick up the second leg of this monumental tour in Ride 2.

LOCAL INFORMATION

♦ D.C. Chamber of Commerce, 1213 K Street N.W., Washington, D.C. 20005, (202) 347–7201.

LOCAL EVENTS/ATTRACTIONS

♦ The John F. Kennedy Center for the Performing Arts, 2700 F Street N.W., Washington, DC 20566; tickets and information (800) 444–1324 or (202) 467–4600; administrative offices: (202) 416–8000; www.kennedy-center.org. The Kennedy Center is a national presidential memorial as well as a performing arts center. Free tours are offered daily, 10:00 A.M. to noon. Charming gift shops and several outstanding restaurants are located in the magnificent building designed by architect Edward Durrell Stone.

♦ Arlington National Cemetery, across Memorial Bridge, about 0.75 mile from Lincoln Memorial, Arlington, VA; www.mdw.army.mil. Open daily 8:00 A.M. to 7:00 P.M., free. America's largest national burial ground, with more than 600 acres of landscaped hills. Among the thousands of white headstones are the graves of President John F. Kennedy, Supreme Court Justice Thurgood Marshall, world champion boxer Joe Louis, and the Tomb of the Unknowns.

Free admission. Choice of self-guided walking tour or paid shuttle tour (information available at visitor center).

◆ Lincoln Memorial, Twenty-third Street between Constitution and Independence Avenues N.W., Washington, D.C.; (202) 426–6841; www.nps.gov. Open daily. There's a gift shop on site. Located on the west end of the National Mall, this memorial was dedicated in 1922 in memory of President Abraham Lincoln. Thirty-eight Grecian columns surround a statue of Lincoln seated atop a 10-foot-high marble base. Lincoln is flanked by engraved readings of the Gettysburg Address, his second inaugural address, and murals by French painter Jules Guerin. The statue sits in quiet repose facing the Reflecting Pool and Washington Monument.

◆ Thomas Jefferson Memorial, Fifteenth Street S.W. on the Tidal Basin, Washington, D.C.; (202) 426–6841; www.nps.gov. Open 8:00 A.M. to midnight daily; closed on December 25. There's a gift shop on site. This dome-shaped rotunda, erected in 1942 as a monument to honor the nation's third president, is in a serene location on the Tidal Basin. Inside, a 19-foot bronze statue of Jefferson stands. The monument is surrounded by a grove of trees, making an especially beautiful scene during cherry blossom season in spring.

ACCOMMODATIONS

◆ Bed & Breakfast Accommodations, P.O. Box 12011, Washington, D.C. 20005; (202) 328–3510; www.bnbaccom.com.

◆ Washington D.C. Accommodations, 2201 Wisconsin Avenue, Suite C110, Washington, D.C. 20007; (202) 289–2220 or (800) 554–2220; www.wdcahotels. com.

BIKE SHOPS

◆ Revolution Cycles, at the foot of Key Bridge, 3411 M Street N.W., Washington, D.C. 20007; (202) 965–3601.

◆ The Bicycle Pro Shop, 3403 M Street N.W., Washington, D.C. 20007; (202) 337–0311.

MAPS

◆ ADC's *Washington Area Bike Map*. Compiled by Metropolitan Washington Council of Governments. $10.95. Available at bookstores and newsstands.

◆ *D.C. Bikeways*. Series of maps published by the city. $3.00. Write to District of Columbia Office of Documents, 441 Fourth Street N.W., Suite 520, Washington, D.C. 20001; (202) 727–5090.

Monuments on the Mall Ramble

T his ramble offers riders the chance to take in some of the
nation's most hallowed monuments from the saddle. The route
covers mostly flat terrain and should take about ninety minutes,
although opportunities to dawdle abound: The Smithsonian and other
museums, the White House, and the Washington Monument are all
part of the tour. The loop's length and lack of hills make it ideal for
beginners, but even intermediate riders will enjoy pedaling past testa-
ments to centuries of U.S. history.

This tour combines the great houses of government with the great houses
of knowledge. I doubt that even Manhattan could boast of such a concentra-
tion of cultural institutions and world-class landmarks.

Begin at the Harry T. Thompson Boat Center (bike rentals available March
to November). If you are arriving by car and parking here, be aware of the
three-hour limit in this metered lot. Proceed to the Lincoln Memorial as
described in Ride 1. Ride to the east steps of the Lincoln Memorial for a stunning view of an axis that includes the Washington Monument and, nearly 2
miles away, the U.S. Capitol.

Head down a slight slope past a souvenir stand on your right to pick up a
path parallel to the 0.5-mile-long Reflecting Pool. Continue past the fountains
(filled with mallard ducklings in spring) and jog to the left on the sidewalk to
reach the pedestrian crossing at busy Seventeenth Street.

Pick up the path leading directly uphill to the Washington Monument,
where a circle of flags always blows stiffly. This high ground is a favored spot
for kite flying. The cornerstone for the 555-foot-tall monument was laid in
1848, but the masonry structure was not completed until 1884. From 9:00 A.M.

Start: Harry T. Thompson Boat Center
Distance: 9.7-mile loop
Approximate pedaling time: 90 minutes
Terrain and surface: Flat except for Capitol Hill; roads and paved paths
Things to see: Washington Monument, Smithsonian museums, U.S. Capitol, Library of Congress, Union Station, the White House, Vietnam Veterans Memorial
Traffic and hazards: Downtown is heavily traveled by cars, buses, trucks—use caution at crossings. The paved paths are safe and wide. No hazards.
Facilities: Rest rooms, gift shops, restaurants, and bike racks at most museums and Union Station
Getting there: From north, Rock Creek Parkway south to Thompson's parking lot; turn right. From Mall, Virginia Avenue west across Rock Creek Parkway to Thompson's parking lot. From Virginia, Theodore Roosevelt Bridge or Memorial Bridge to Rock Creek Parkway to Thompson's parking lot. By Metro, Blue or Orange Line to Foggy Bottom/GWU, about a 1-mile walk or ride. From Metro station, walk south on Twenty-third Street (away from Washington Circle). Turn right onto H Street, left onto New Hampshire Avenue, and right onto Virginia Avenue. Cross Rock Creek Parkway at crosswalk to reach parking lot of Thompson Boat Center. Follow one-lane road over short bridge to waterfront.

to 5:00 P.M. (until midnight in spring and summer), you can ride the elevator up to the 500-foot level (call ahead).

Back on your bike, continue downhill past a souvenir stand on a path to Fifteenth Street. Cross carefully and take another path to a signal at Fourteenth Street. Dismount and cross to one-way Jefferson Drive, the starting point for a tour of the south side of the National Mall. Conceived by Pierre L'Enfant as a residential boulevard, the Mall was densely planted as a romantic forest in the 1800s and streamlined as a grassy, elm-lined promenade in the early 1900s. It is the home of nine Smithsonian museums plus the National Gallery of Art, an ice-skating rink, and a building of the Department of Agriculture. All museums are free.

Your first stop is the recently renovated Freer Museum, the first Smithsonian art museum, dating from 1923. Housed in a building styled after an Italian palace, the Freer collection devotes itself to Asian art, particularly jade sculpture, lacquers, and porcelain. Not to be missed is the ornate Peacock Room, which was moved intact from art patron Charles Freer's Detroit mansion along with more than a hundred artworks by James Abbott McNeill Whistler.

The next few hundred feet feature: the turreted Smithsonian Castle, a romantic brownstone structure designed by the architect of St. Patrick's Cathedral; the Arts & Industries Building, a High Victorian pile exhibiting American technology as it existed in 1876; the doughnut-shaped Hirshhorn Museum and its outdoor sculpture garden, both devoted to modern art; and the National Air and Space Museum,

The Washington Monument

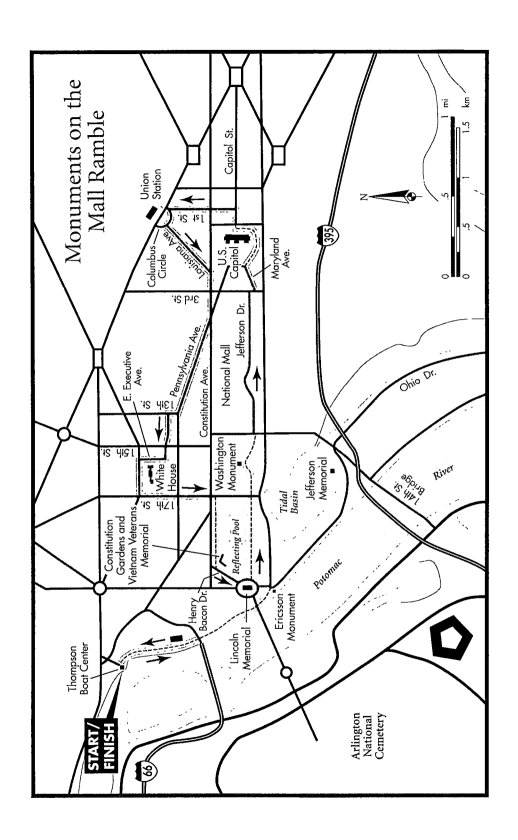

Monuments on the Mall Ramble

Union Station

Capitol St.

1st St.

Columbus Circle

Louisiana Ave.

U.S. Capitol

3rd St.

Maryland Ave.

Jefferson Dr.

395

N

1 mi

km

.5

1

1.5

.5

1

.5

0

0

E. Executive Ave.

Pennsylvania Ave.

Constitution Ave.

National Mall

13th St.

15th St.

White House

17th St.

Washington Monument

Tidal Basin

Jefferson Memorial

Ohio Dr.

14th St. Bridge

River

Constitution Gardens and Vietnam Veterans Memorial

Reflecting Pool

Henry Bacon Dr.

Lincoln Memorial

Ericsson Monument

Potomac

Thompson Boat Center

START/FINISH

66

Arlington National Cemetery

Note: Use blocks and features to navigate instead of miles.

♦ From the Thompson Boat Center parking area, turn right onto bike path (Potomac River is on your right).

♦ Proceed 1.5 miles to Ericsson Monument. Turn left to head up short road (sign reads TAXIS ONLY) to Lincoln Memorial.

♦ Facing east toward the Capitol building, pick up bike path parallel to Reflecting Pool. Proceed 0.5 mile to Seventeenth Street pedestrian crossing (traffic signal).

♦ Take path short distance east (uphill) to Washington Monument. Proceed on bike/foot paths across Fifteenth and Fourteenth Streets to Jefferson Drive. Begin tour of south side of National Mall.

♦ Follow Jefferson Drive about 0.5 mile along the Mall. Detour here for the shorter version. Otherwise, turn right onto Third Street and quickly left onto Maryland Avenue. Proceed past statue of James Garfield to U.S. Capitol grounds.

♦ Follow footpaths around south side of Capitol building to east front. Proceed to East Capitol Street. Pass through stone gates; go left on First Street.

♦ If interested in the Capitol Hill detour, ride 1 block to East Capitol Street, turn right, and pick up those directions. Otherwise, take First Street about 0.75 mile to Columbus Circle in front of Union Station. Turn right on circle and left onto service road in front of station. Watch out for traffic in this busy area.

♦ Exit station area on service road; turn left. Take second right onto Louisiana Avenue.

♦ Proceed less than 1 mile past parks and bell tower. Take oblique right onto Constitution Avenue. In 2 blocks turn right onto Pennsylvania Avenue (heavy traffic except on weekends).

♦ In 11 blocks, turn right onto Thirteenth Street and quick left onto Pennsylvania Avenue North. Pass National Theater and Willard Hotel to reach Fifteenth Street. Cross at signal to continue straight on Hamilton Place. Walk bike on sidewalk.

♦ In about one half block, turn right through gates onto East Executive Avenue. Exit through another set of gates; turn left past White House. Cross at Seventeenth Street signal and turn left.

♦ Ride 3 long blocks to Constitution Avenue. Cross at signal and pick up bike path (west) past Constitution Gardens and Vietnam Veterans Memorial.

♦ Return up Henry Bacon Drive to Lincoln Memorial. Return to Ericsson statue and retrace route to the Thompson Boat Center.

Option: North Side of Mall Elective

This route stays on the Mall and avoids some heavily trafficked roads. It also shaves several miles from the trip while affording a chance to see the Mall's other four museums: the National Gallery (East Building and West Building, featuring dramatically

(continued)

different collections), the Museum of Natural History, and the Museum of American History, which features an interesting selection of antique bicycles—not to mention a seminude statue of George Washington.

Directions from Jefferson Drive:

◆ Left onto Third Street.
◆ Left onto Madison Drive (one way).
◆ Straight onto Fourteenth Street. Cross to Washington Monument grounds.
◆ Straight to Seventeenth Street. Cross to path parallel to Constitution Avenue.
◆ Follow signs to Constitution Gardens and Vietnam Veterans Memorial.
◆ Follow path to Lincoln Memorial.

Option: Capitol Hill Detour:

This 2-mile side trip through a Victorian row-house neighborhood takes you past the homes of many members of Congress. Be sure to stop at Eastern Market, an old-fashioned farmers' market at Seventh Street and North Carolina Avenue, for a late breakfast or lunch.

From east front of U.S. Capitol:

◆ Straight on East Capitol Street, 11 blocks to Lincoln Park.
◆ Turn right onto Eleventh Street.
◆ In 1 block, turn right onto North Carolina Avenue.
◆ After stopping at Eastern Market, proceed on North Carolina to Pennsylvania Avenue. Turn right.
◆ Left onto Independence Avenue at Second Street. Take first right onto First Street. Proceed 5 long blocks to Union Station to pick up the route.

which is the nation's most visited museum (9.5 million people annually). Within this great hangarlike structure you can find everything from the *Spirit of St. Louis* to space modules used in the Apollo-Soyuz project. Almost everyone takes in a 70-millimeter IMAX film, shown on the Langley Theater's five-story screen.

If you stop to dawdle at the Castle, don't miss the Smithsonian's newest museums: the National Museum of African Art and the Arthur M. Sackler Gallery, devoted to Asian art. Both are located beneath a landscaped plaza facing Independence Avenue.

If you are following the shorter, North Side of Mall Elective (recommended for those not comfortable cycling on urban streets), pick up those directions at this point. Continuing east, leave Jefferson Drive at Third Street to enter Maryland Avenue. On the right stands the U.S. Botanical Gardens, a Victorian-style greenhouse filled with tropical orchids and blooming cacti. Unless you take the shorter alternate route to see the Mall's north side (see Miles and Directions) the next stop is what L'Enfant called Congress House.

Started in 1793, burned in 1814, finished in 1867, and constantly updated since, the U.S. Capitol is situated on one of Washington's highest hills. In the 1870s it was landscaped by Frederick Law Olmsted, the principal designer of Manhattan's Central Park. The grounds retain odd little additions such as Japanese lanterns, a grotto, and a trolley stop. Follow a looping path to the Capitol's east side for views of the Library of Congress and the Supreme Court; then turn left onto First Street. Follow First Street to where it intersects with East Capitol Street. You have the option to ride through the Capitol Hill neighborhood and visit a farmers' market at this point. If interested, turn right and pick up the directions for the Capitol Hill Detour from here. Otherwise, continue straight on First Street and you will soon arrive at Union Station. Long empty and decaying, the 1907 station reopened in 1988 as a shopping mall after a painstaking $100 million restoration. Its Roman-inspired architecture matches that of just about any of D.C.'s great public buildings. Best of all, it still serves Amtrak, Metrorail, and commuter trains. Union Station features well-designed and well-located bike racks, so it's a good place to park the eighteen-speed and explore the city on foot or by rail.

After touring the grand station, exit the area via Louisiana Avenue, cutting diagonally southwest. Within 4 blocks you'll meet Constitution Avenue. Turn right and in 2 blocks start cruising down the Avenue of the Presidents— Pennsylvania Avenue. Since the time of Thomas Jefferson, this 1-mile stretch has hosted the inaugural parade. Until recently, the street's seedy demeanor belied its importance. But a $1 billion effort since 1976 has resulted in four new parks and memorials, restoration of several major landmarks, and construction of new hotels, offices, and restaurants. On weekends the boulevard is lightly traveled. Don't miss the new Navy War Memorial, the Canadian Chancery, the National Archives, the FBI Building (open for a rat-a-tat of a tour), and the restored Old (1897) Post Office, with its 315-foot bell tower and pavilion filled with shops. At Thirteenth Street, Pennsylvania Avenue splits into north and south. Follow the ride directions until you reach a plaza anchored by a statue of Alexander Hamilton.

After 1 block, turn right through the gates onto East Executive Avenue, a landscaped lane flanking the White House. Walk your bike—there is always a crowd of people lining up for tours of the White House. Here an elaborate security system has been disguised to maintain the aesthetics of the grounds.

Passing through the gateway at the other end, turn left to arrive at 1600 Pennsylvania Avenue N.W., the address of every American president since John Adams. Designed by Irish-born architect James Hoban, the White House was painted its alabaster hue to cover damage caused by the British burning of 1814. Pennsylvania Avenue fronting the White House was closed to vehicular

The bike paths make it easy to get to a rugby game.

traffic in 1995. Drivers grumbled at the time, but walkers, joggers, in-line skaters, and cyclists have since turned this most famous stretch of street into a festive, car-free promenade.

Just past the White House on the right stands Blair-Lee House, a kind of guest house for the White House. You can usually tell who is visiting by the color of the flags flying. Next door is the Renwick Gallery, a Smithsonian museum devoted to objects made by contemporary American artisans.

Carefully picking your way through one of Washington's busiest intersections, turn left onto Seventeenth Street. Pass another fine art museum, the Corcoran Gallery, and the Organization of American States Building. Continue south to reach Constitution Avenue, a grand esplanade built on top of the old city canal. The last vestige of the canal, which was an open sewer as much as a waterway, is the old lock keeper's house at Seventeenth and Constitution. Cross the road to find a winding path to the right to Constitution Gardens, a fifty-acre park dedicated in 1976. It features 5,000 trees, including honey locust, dogwood, and maple, and a seven-and-a-half-acre lake that is home to carp, turtles, mallards, and geese.

Follow signs to the Vietnam Veterans Memorial. Designed by twenty-one-year-old architecture student Maya Lin, who won an open competition, the memorial features the names of more than 58,000 soldiers inscribed on a wall of polished black granite. In 1993 the Vietnam Women's Memorial by sculptor Glenna Goodacre was added to honor the work of the women Vietnam veterans. Expect crowds, flowers, tears. Signs forbid you to bring your bike right up to "The Wall." Proceed up Henry Bacon Drive back to the Lincoln Memorial and double back to the Thompson Boat Center.

LOCAL INFORMATION

♦ D.C. Chamber of Commerce, 1213 K Street N.W., Washington, D.C. 20005; (202) 347–7201.

LOCAL EVENTS/ATTRACTIONS

♦ Washington Monument, Constitution Avenue and Fifteenth Street N.W., Washington, D.C.; (202) 426–6841; www.nps.gov/wash. Open 9:00 A.M. to 4:45 P.M.; closed December 25. This majestic obelisk is one of the tallest masonry structures in the world. The monument is a memorial to George Washington, our nation's first president, and was dedicated in 1885. It took forty years to complete its construction due to lack of funds. In order to enter the Washington Monument, tickets are required. Free tickets are distributed by the National Park Service for same-day visits from the kiosk on the Washington Monument grounds at Fifteenth Street and Madison Drive on a first-come, first-served basis. Hours for the ticket kiosk are 8:30 A.M. to 4:30 P.M., but tickets run out early. Advance tickets are available for $1.50 service fee per ticket, plus a 50-cent handling fee per order. Call (800) 967–2283 or visit reservations. nps.gov.
♦ Korean War Veterans Memorial, Daniel French Drive and Independence Avenue S.W., Washington, D.C.; (202) 426–6841, www.nps.gov. Open 8:00 A.M. to 11:45 P.M. Our nation honors her daughters and sons who answered the call during the Korean War (1950–1953) at one of the newest memorials in Washington. Nineteen figures representing every ethnic background move toward victory in Korea. They are supported by a dark gray granite wall of 2,400 faces of land, sea, and air support troops. A Pool of Remembrance with the names of the Allied Forces at the base honors all who were killed, captured, wounded, or remain missing in action.
♦ Lincoln Memorial, Twenty-third Street between Constitution and Independence Avenues N.W., Washington, D.C.; (202) 426–6841; www.nps.gov. Open daily. There's a gift shop on site. Located on the west end of the National Mall, this memorial was dedicated in 1922 in memory of President Abraham Lincoln. Thirty-eight Grecian columns surround a statue of Lincoln seated atop a 10-foot-high marble base. Lincoln is flanked by engraved readings of the Gettysburg Address, his second inaugural address, and murals by French painter Jules Guerin. The statue sits in quiet repose facing the Reflecting Pool and the Washington Monument.
♦ Thomas Jefferson Memorial, Fifteenth Street S.W. on the Tidal Basin, Washington, D.C.; (202) 426–6841; www.nps.gov. Open 8:00 A.M. to midnight daily;

closed December 25. There's a gift shop on site. This dome-shaped rotunda, erected in 1942 as a monument to honor the nation's third president, is in a serene location on the Tidal Basin. Inside, a 19-foot bronze statue of Jefferson stands. The monument is surrounded by a grove of trees, making an especially beautiful scene during cherry blossom season in spring.

♦ Vietnam Veterans Memorial, Constitution Avenue and Henry Bacon Drive N.W., Washington, D.C.; (202) 634–1568; www.nps.gov. Open daily 8:00 A.M. to 11:45 P.M., except December 25. The black granite walls of this moving V-shaped memorial are inscribed with the names of the 58,209 Americans missing or killed in the Vietnam conflict. Across the lawn is Frederick Hart's life-size bronze sculpture depicting three young servicemen.

ACCOMMODATIONS

♦ Bed & Breakfast Accommodations, P.O. Box 12011, Washington, D.C. 20005; (202) 328–3510; www.bnbaccom.com.
♦ Washington D.C. Accommodations, 2201 Wisconsin Avenue, Suite C110, Washington, D.C. 20007; (202) 289–2220 or (800) 554–2220; www.wdcahotels. com.

BIKE SHOPS

♦ Revolution Cycles, at the foot of Key Bridge, 3411 M Street N.W., Washington, D.C. 20007; (202) 965–3601.
♦ The Bicycle Pro Shop, 3403 M Street N.W., Washington, D.C. 20007; (202) 337–0311.

MAPS

♦ ADC's Washington Area Bike Map. Compiled by Metropolitan Washington Council of Governments. $10.95. Available at bookstores and newsstands.
♦ D.C. Bikeways. Series of maps published by the city. $3.00. Write to District of Columbia Office of Documents, 441 Fourth Street N.W., Suite 520, Washington, D.C. 20001; (202) 727–5090.

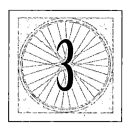

Rock Creek Park Ramble

D.C.

Rock Creek Park is an oasis of nearly untarnished nature amid the hustle and bustle of the nation's capital. Just a stone's throw from the busy Georgetown district, riders can pedal alongside a pristine creek and, on weekends, enjoy a break from urban traffic on long stretches of road that are closed to cars. The only potential drawback for those who take advantage of the park's closed roads during the weekend are the hordes of like-minded cyclists, in-line skaters, and joggers, who can make some parts of the route a bit congested.

In 1863 the naturalist John Burroughs wrote, "There is perhaps not another city in the Union that has on its threshold so much natural beauty and grandeur, such as men seek for in remote forests and mountains. A few touches of art would convert this whole region into a park unequalled in the world." The area he referred to was north of settled Washington, a forested place full of glens and meadows and ferns.

A few years later the U.S. Army Corps of Engineers surveyed the same area, seeking a healthful new site for the White House. Instead they recommended that Rock Creek would make an excellent city greensward. Finally, in 1890, Burroughs's wish came true when Congress created 1,800-acre Rock Creek Park in the Northwest quadrant.

Today this stream valley once inhabited by the Algonquins provides recreation for many of D.C.'s 570,000 residents. In addition to boulder-strewn Rock Creek, it contains several other streams, tennis courts, hiking and bridle trails, a nature center, planetarium, and historic buildings. The park provides an excellent commuting route for bikers from the neighborhoods of Cleveland Park, Woodley Park, Mount Pleasant, and Adams-Morgan to downtown D.C.

Wrought iron and stunning masonry are sprinkled throughout the ride.

The park also provides a sanctuary for more wildlife than you might expect in the heart of a city. Look for mallards, wood ducks, and even a family of black-crowned night herons in the creek. You may also spot raccoons, foxes, deer, and beavers nearby.

A tour of Rock Creek Park begins at the creek's mouth on the Potomac. You can rent a bike (or a canoe or rowing shell) at the Harry T. Thompson Boat Center just off Virginia Avenue and Rock Creek Parkway N.W. Thompson's (open March to November) also has bike racks, lockers, water fountains, and rest rooms.

Leaving Thompson's, with the Watergate Apartment complex and Kennedy Center on your right, turn left on the path heading north. Note on the right, on the other side of the Rock Creek Parkway and beneath a freeway ramp, the ruins of the Godey lime kiln, a vestige of a prosperous nineteenth-century industry. The path winds along the parkway for the next 3 miles, at times almost grazing the road and then disappearing into thickets of woods. It crosses Rock Creek five times on bridges.

An exercise course parallels the route. On a spring day the path becomes an olio of humanity, with Lycra-clad runners and cyclists mingling with baby strollers, birders, and groups of Chinese from the nearby embassy of the People's Republic. You'll even see children fishing and wading in the creek. In spring the embankment blazes with thousands of jonquils, daffodils, and tulips, while the woods bloom with dogwoods and redbud. In addition to the bright shades of crimson and yellow provided by these flora, the park always seems cool, green, and mossy thanks to its many trees and rock formations. The boulders that turn Rock Creek into cascades and provide dramatic outcroppings in the valley are the same type of Potomac Bluestone carved into building stone for the visitor center and handsomely crafted retaining walls within the park.

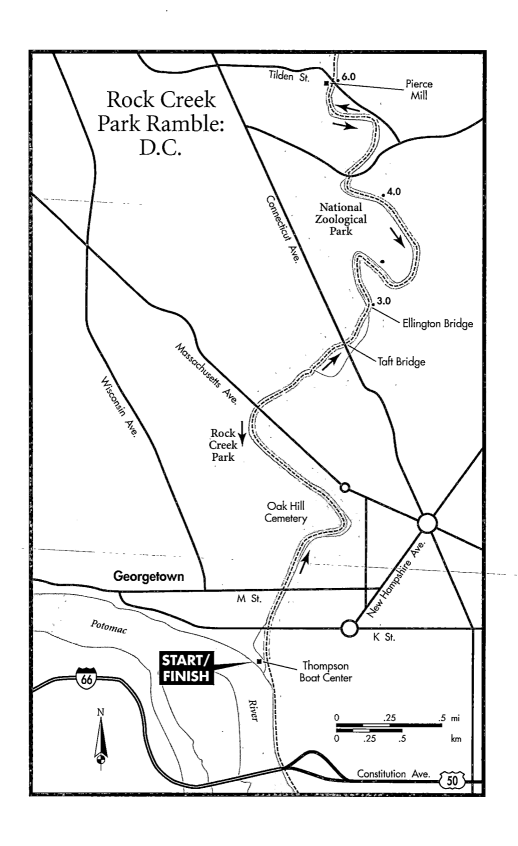

Rock Creek Park Ramble: D.C.

Tilden St.
6.0
Pierce Mill

Connecticut Ave.

4.0

National Zoological Park

3.0

Ellington Bridge

Massachusetts Ave.

Taft Bridge

Wisconsin Ave.

Rock Creek Park

Oak Hill Cemetery

New Hampshire Ave.

Georgetown

M St.

Potomac

K St.

66

START/ FINISH

Thompson Boat Center

River

N

| 0 | .25 | .5 mi |
| 0 | .25 | .5 | km |

Constitution Ave.

50

0.0 From Thompson Boat Center, cross one-lane short bridge to parking lot.

0.25 From parking lot, take curb cut at left to join Rock Creek Trail.

1.75 After passing exercise course, dismount and cross Rock Creek Parkway at crosswalk.

3.0 Bear right at fork in trail and ride under arches of Ellington Bridge.

3.5 At tunnel, turn left and ride through gate to path bordering Rock Creek.

4.0 At service road crossing, turn left to ride over stone bridge into National Zoo. Return to trail via stone bridge. Turn left to head north.

6.0 At parking lot near waterfall, turn left to visit Pierce Mill and Art Barn. Return to trail to join rides described in Ride 4, Ride 5, or Ride 11. To return to Thompson Boat Center, turn around and retrace steps.

Passing under the decks of several old auto bridges, you pedal next to Oak Hill Cemetery, a twelve-acre burial ground founded in 1849 and filled with ornate Victorian monuments. As you pass under the Dumbarton Bridge, note the Indian heads carved in sandstone. This is also near the site of Lyons Mill, which was built in 1780 but collapsed with a roar in 1913. The stone piers for the bike-path bridge are all that remain of what was once Rock Creek's biggest industry.

After carefully crossing three parkway entrance ramps, you will thread under the Taft Bridge (1909) and then the Ellington Bridge (1935), named for jazz musician Duke Ellington and identifiable by three graceful arches rising 150 feet from the creek basin. Bear right on the path to travel under one of those arches. After crossing a small bridge with a narrow sidewalk, come to a parkway tunnel that contains an even slenderer path. Avoid the tunnel by turning left onto a smooth path parallel to Rock Creek. Glide over a stone bridge to the left to arrive at the National Zoological Park.

Founded in 1890 and laid out by Frederick Law Olmsted, the first landscape architect in the United States and designer of Central Park in New York City, the 163-acre zoo features hundreds of species of reptiles and mammals, including a giant panda and golden tamarind monkeys. Bicycle riding is not allowed in the zoo, but you can park your bike (locked securely!) or walk it to any of the nearby exhibits. Lately the zoo has been developing what it calls BioParks, which are realistic and edifying replicas of diverse ecosystems. In 1992 the zoo realized this concept by building Amazonia, a $12 million rain-forest exhibition under a climate-controlled dome.

Back on the trail, you wind along through hardwood forest and dense alder bushes for a mile or so (be sure to check the creek for wood ducks and kingfishers) until arriving at Pierce Mill, the last of eight water-powered mills once driven by Rock Creek.

Built about 1820 from blue granite, the mill was restored in 1985 by the National Park Service. You once could buy buckwheat and cornmeal ground on site through a remarkable system of millstones, wooden gears, shafts, hoppers, and chutes. However, the milling equipment broke in 1993; the Friends of Pierce Mill (8404 Pittsfield Court, Potomac, MD 20854; 202–244–2378) are raising funds in hopes of restoring it to working order. Close by are picnic grounds, rest rooms, and the Art Barn, a gallery installed in a former carriage house.

Continue north to the Pierce Mill parking lot. On weekends and holidays this is the starting place for an exhilarating 10-mile round trip on Beach Drive, closed to traffic. But on weekdays, the road reverts to a major commuter byway, and though it is marked an on-road bike path, I don't recommend it. If you're making this tour on a weekday, return to Thompson's the way you came. The remainder of Rock Creek Park is a treat best saved for weekends. To add about 8 miles, combine this ride with Ride 11 (Upper Reaches of Rock Creek Park).

On the trip back, the first bridge you traverse is a concrete span stamped 1982. Look to the left across the road to view a bench carved from granite and inscribed JUSSERAND—PERSONAL TRIBUTE OF ESTEEM AND AFFECTION—1855–1932. (Jusserand was a French ambassador and friend of Teddy Roosevelt.)

LOCAL INFORMATION

♦ D.C. Chamber of Commerce, 1213 K Street N.W., Washington, D.C. 20005; (202) 347–7201
♦ Conference and Visitors Bureau of Montgomery County, MD, Inc., 11820 Parklawn Drive, Suite 380, Rockville, MD 20852; (301) 428–9702 or (800) 925–0880.
♦ Montgomery County Recreation Department, 12210 Bushey Drive, Silver Spring, MD 20902; (240) 777–6804 (general information—recording).

LOCAL EVENTS/ATTRACTIONS

♦ Rock Creek Park, Washington, D.C.; www.nps.gov. Luckily for Washingtonians, in 1890 Congress prevented this 1,800-acre green valley that cuts a swathe from Georgetown north through the city to the Maryland state line from becoming the unofficial city dump. Today this tranquil urban valley is a haven for bikers, joggers, and picnickers. It is a place where people can enjoy themselves, sitting quietly under the shade trees along the banks of the creek, cooking over a barbecue grill, or enjoying the sight and fragrance of the daffodils and other flowers that bloom here each spring.
♦ Rock Creek Park Nature Center & Planetarium, 5200 Glover Road N.W., Washington, D.C.; (202) 426–6829. A spot where you can see live and mounted wildlife displays, environmental exhibits, planetarium shows and participate in

guided nature walks. For horseback riding lessons, visit the Horse Centre off Military Road at 5100 Glover Road N.W.; (202) 362–0117.

♦ National Zoological Park, 3001 Connecticut Avenue N.W., Washington, D.C.; (202) 673–4717; www.natzoo.si.edu. Open May 1 to September 15, grounds: 6:00 A.M. to 8:00 P.M., buildings: 10:00 A.M. to 6:00 P.M.; September 16 to April 30, grounds 6:00 A.M. to 6:00 P.M., buildings: 10:00 A.M. to 4:30 P.M. (closed December 25). Thousands of animals, including many endangered species. Amazonia is a recreated microcosm of the world's largest rain forest. The National Zoo is now the home of two pandas, Mei Xiang and Tian Tian.

ACCOMMODATIONS

♦ Bed & Breakfast Accommodations, P.O. Box 12011, Washington, D.C. 20005; (202) 328–3510, www.bnbaccom.com.

♦ Washington D.C. Accommodations, 2201 Wisconsin Avenue, Suite C110, Washington, D.C. 20007; (202) 289–2220 or (800) 554–2220; www.wdcahotels. com.

♦ Bethesda Marriott Hotel, 5151 Pooks Hill Road, Bethesda MD 20814; (301) 897–9400 or (800) 228–9290; fax (301) 897–4165.

♦ Holiday Inn Select Bethesda, 8120 Wisconsin Avenue, Bethesda, MD 20814; (301) 652–2000 or (800) HOLIDAY; fax: (301) 652–4525.

BIKE SHOPS

♦ Revolution Cycles, at the foot of Key Bridge, 3411 M Street N.W., Washington, D.C. 20007; (202) 965–3601.

♦ The Bicycle Pro Shop, 3403 M Street N.W., Washington, D.C. 20007; (202) 337–0311.

MAPS

♦ *ADC's Washington Area Bike Map*. Compiled by Metropolitan Washington Council of Governments. $10.95. Available at bookstores and newsstands.

♦ *D.C. Bikeways*. Series of maps published by the city. $3.00. Write to District of Columbia Office of Documents, 441 Fourth Street N.W., Suite 520, Washington, D.C. 20001; (202) 727–5090.

♦ *Maryland Bicycle Touring Map*. Free. Available from Office of Tourism Development, 45 Calvert Street, Annapolis, MD 21401.

♦ *Trails in Montgomery County Parks*. Contact Maryland–National Capital Park and Planning Commission (MNCPPC), 8787 Georgia Avenue N.W., Silver Spring, MD 20910; (301) 495–2503; www.mncppc.org.

Rock Creek Park Ramble

TO MARYLAND AND BACK

Thistramble will take you on a journey out of the city and, seemingly, into the wilderness—all in the short span of the ride! The northern reaches of Rock Creek Park are known to be some of the most beautiful in the D.C. area. You will find serene Japanese pagodas, awestriking spires atop a Mormon temple, and the surreal solitude of nature a mere bike ride away from the busy streets of D.C.

In the 1970s the National Park Service agreed to a bold experiment. On weekends and holidays, Beach Drive, one of the busiest roads leading into Rock Creek Park, would be closed to motorized traffic.

Perhaps to the pleasant surprise of the men in green, park use actually increased on auto-free days. So the park service institutionalized 7:00 A.M. to 7:00 P.M. closings of portions of the road. Meanwhile, an off-road trail was paved through the 2,700-acre Maryland section of Rock Creek Regional Park, providing an uninterrupted 12.5-mile ride from Pierce Mill in D.C. to Viers Mill in Maryland. The trail also extends 5 miles farther north to Lake Needwood, where pedalboats and canoes may be rented in summertime.

This route is organized as a round trip combining pathway and roadway travel. If you are nervous about cars, stick to the paths, but expect competition from strollers and pets.

The northern D.C. section of Rock Creek is flat-out gorgeous. Riding along a two-lane parkway designed to provide great vistas of hardwood forests and rushing waters, you can easily imagine yourself a hundred miles from the city.

Art Barn, Viers Mill

Start: Pierce Mill parking lot

Distance: 27-mile loop

Approximate pedaling time: 2–3 hours

Terrain and surface: Rolling; smooth roads closed to cars weekends and holidays, on-road routes, and paved off-road paths

Things to see: Ravines of upper Rock Creek, Walter Reed Annex, Mormon Temple and gardens, Kensington antiques center, Woodend estate, Miller Cabin, Pierce Mill

Traffic and hazards: Closed to traffic on weekends and holidays. Well-kept surfaces.

Facilities: Rest rooms at Pierce Mill, park service substation, and Meadowbrook Park; food and antiques shops in Kensington; gift shop at Woodend

Getting there: Heading south on Connecticut Avenue, turn left onto Tilden Street to Pierce Mill parking lot. From Rock Creek Parkway, head north to Tilden Street; turn left to Pierce Mill parking lot. From Sixteenth Street, take Piney Branch Parkway west to Pierce Mill parking lot. By Metro, take Red Line to Cleveland Park station, then ride 0.25 mile to Tilden Street; turn right to Pierce Mill parking lot.

After crossing East-West High-way, pick up an off-road trail that leads you under the remains of an old Baltimore & Ohio train trestle and through wetlands and stands of evergreens. Bear right where the Georgetown Branch Trail intersects. After passing a small playground, turn right to detour uphill on an old footpath to the Walter Reed Army Medical Center Annex, a fascinating and eccentric campus on a high hill.

Built as a women's seminary nearly a century ago and annexed by the army during World War II, the 190-acre complex is almost like a pop-up sampler of world architecture. There's a Japanese pagoda, a Dutch windmill, a 600-year-old Roman fountain, a Bavarian resort hotel with stained-glass windows, and dormitory buildings that wouldn't look out of place in seventeenth-century Brussels. The idea was to provide the female seminarians with the sophistication afforded by world travel without exposing them to worldly evils. Unfortunately, the army says the badly deteriorating buildings will be torn down. Although preservationists promise a spirited fight, I wouldn't wait too long to see this architectural oddity. (For more information, contact Save Our Seminary at Forest Glen, P.O. Box 8274, Silver Spring, MD 20907, or check the Web site at www.operant.com/Seminary.)

The next point of interest, accessible from Stoneybrook Road, is the Washington Temple for the Church of Jesus Christ of the Latter-Day Saints. Soaring upright from a field of electric-green grass, the temple's profile from afar has been compared to Dorothy's first sighting of Oz. One of forty-one Mormon temples worldwide reserved for sacred ceremonies such as marriages and baptisms, the gleaming structure of white Alabama marble was completed in 1974. It rises 288 feet to a gold-plated statue of the angel Moroni. The temple is closed to non-Mormons, but you can see photos of the sanctum sanctorum in the visitor center. The fifty-six-acre grounds are also worth a look.

Back on the trail, head west parallel to the creek through residential neighborhoods. At a four-way stop, take a right onto Kensington Parkway to visit the town of Kensington, a Victorian streetcar suburb with grand old frame houses and many antiques shops. After taking tea at the Country Cupboard Tea Room (3750 Howard Avenue, Kensington, MD 20895; 301–933–1226), return to the path to head north to Viers Mill, a county park.

Ride back to D.C. on Jones Mill Road and Beach Drive for different scenery and sights. This route affords a chance to see Woodend, the headquarters of the Audubon Naturalist Society of the Central Atlantic States. The forty-acre estate is cultivated to provide a variety of habitats that have attracted rabbits, bullfrogs, woodpeckers, and even wild turkeys to the midst of this suburban area. There's also a formal garden and a Georgian mansion, which contains a shop selling books, calendars, binoculars, toys, and bird feeders. I find this shop particularly useful before Christmas. While the rest of Washington fumes in shopping traffic, I'm playing Santa with spokes, pedaling off to Woodend to stuff my panniers with gifts. Look closely for Woodend's small sign—it's easy to miss.

Back on a narrow, winding road lined with bungalows, you soon come to an intersection with Jones Bridge Road. About 20 yards past the intersection is the Georgetown Branch Trail. This disused freight line is part of what local hikers and bikers hope will become a fully paved, 11-mile path linking Silver Spring, Maryland, with Georgetown and the C & O Canal National Historic Park. The stretch here is part of the hard-packed gravel path between Silver Spring and Bethesda; it connects with the paved Capital Crescent Trail, which runs between Bethesda and Georgetown. It's at the heart of this book's next ride, Capital Crescent Ramble.

The return to Pierce Mill via Beach Drive is almost all downhill. Keep an eye out for crow-size pileated woodpeckers attacking the hardwood trees lining this winding road. Also, several miles down Beach Drive, take a look at the former home of Joaquin Miller, the "Poet of the Sierras," who lived in Washington in the 1880s. Located on the west side of Beach Drive, it is reputed to be the only log cabin in D.C. The Miller Cabin hosts poetry readings on many summer nights.

LOCAL INFORMATION

♦ D.C. Chamber of Commerce, 1213 K Street N.W., Washington, D.C. 20005; (202) 347–7201.
♦ Conference and Visitors Bureau of Montgomery County, Maryland, Inc., 11820 Parklawn Drive, Suite 380, Rockville, MD 20852; (301) 428–9702 or (800) 925–0880.
♦ Montgomery County Recreation Department, 12210 Bushey Drive, Silver Spring, MD 20902, (240) 777–6804 (general information recording).

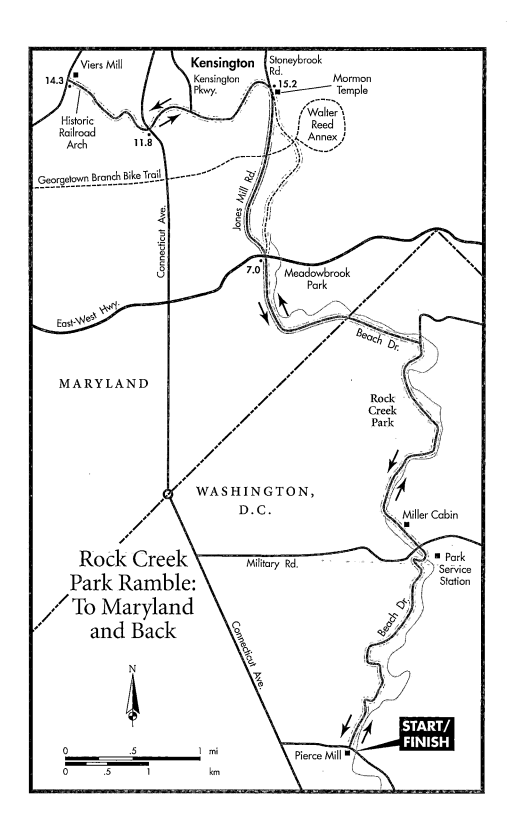

Viers Mill

14.3 ■

Kensington

Kensington
Pkwy.

Stoneybrook
Rd.

■ **15.2**

Mormon
Temple

Historic
Railroad
Arch

11.8

Walter
Reed
Annex

Georgetown Branch Bike Trail

Jones Mill Rd.

Connecticut Ave.

7.0

Meadowbrook
Park

East-West Hwy.

Beach Dr.

MARYLAND

Rock
Creek
Park

WASHINGTON,
D.C.

Miller Cabin ■

Rock Creek
Park Ramble:
To Maryland
and Back

Military Rd.

■ Park
Service
Station

Connecticut Ave.

Beach Dr.

N

**START/
FINISH**

0	.5	1	mi
0	.5	1	km

Pierce Mill ■

0.0	From Pierce Mill parking area, head north on path, with creek to your right.
0.5	Pass through auto barriers (weekends only) to enter Beach Drive. Stay on Beach Drive north past D.C. line. Follow bike-route signs, turning right over narrow wooden bridge at Meadowbrook Park, then left around park and past Meadowbrook stables.
7.0	Cross East-West Highway at traffic light to pick up off-road trail. Bear right where Georgetown Branch Trail intersects with bike path. (Ride 5 may be picked up at this point.)
8.0	Pass small playground, then take optional right turn up zigzag path to Walter Reed Annex.
11.4	Stay on path to Kensington Parkway (four-way stop). (**Option:** Turn right for 2.8-mile round trip detour to historic Kensington.)
14.3	Return to path and turn right. Continue to Viers Mill and turn around. (**Option:** Continue 5 miles north to Lake Needwood.) To return on road, turn left onto Beach Drive.
15.2	Pass Mormon Temple; then right on unmarked Jones Mill Road. Watch for Woodend sign; right on steep drive to explore estate.
18.5	Return to Jones Mill. At intersection with Jones Bridge Road, continue straight. Note Georgetown Branch Trail connection just 20 yards past intersection. Continue down Jones Mill Road, which turns into Beach Drive after East-West Highway intersection.
27	Beach Drive back to Pierce Mill.

LOCAL EVENTS/ATTRACTIONS

♦ Rock Creek Park, Washington, D.C.; www.nps.gov. Luckily for Washingtonians, in 1890 Congress prevented this 1,800-acre green valley that cuts a swathe from Georgetown north through the city to the Maryland state line from becoming the unofficial city dump. Today this tranquil urban valley is a haven for bikers, joggers, and picnickers. It is a place where people can enjoy themselves, sitting quietly under the shade trees along the banks of the creek, cooking over a barbecue grill, or enjoying the sight and fragrance of the daffodils and other flowers that bloom here each spring.

♦ Rock Creek Park Nature Center & Planetarium, 5200 Glover Road N.W., Washington, D.C.; (202) 426–6829. A spot where you can see live and mounted wildlife displays, environmental exhibits, and planetarium shows, as well as participate in guided nature walks. For horseback-riding lessons, visit the Horse Centre off Military Road at 5100 Glover Road N.W. Call (202) 362–0117.

♦ National Zoological Park, 3001 Connecticut Avenue N.W., Washington, D.C. (202) 673–4717; www.natzoo.si.edu. From May 1 through September 15, the grounds are open from 6:00 A.M. to 8:00 P.M., the buildings from 10:00 A.M. to 6:00 P.M. From September 16 through April 30, the grounds are open from 6:00 A.M. to 6:00 P.M., the buildings from 10:00 A.M. to 4:30 P.M. Closed December 25. Thousands of animals, including many endangered species. Amazonia is a re-created microcosm of the world's largest rain forest. The National Zoo is now the home of two pandas, Mei Xiang and Tian Tian.

ACCOMMODATIONS

♦ Bed & Breakfast Accommodations, P.O. Box 12011, Washington, D.C.; (202) 328–3510; www.bnbaccom.com.
♦ Washington D.C. Accommodations, 2201 Wisconsin Avenue, Suite C110, Washington, D.C. 20007; (202) 289–2220 or (800) 554–2220; www.wdcahotels. com.
♦ Bethesda Marriott Hotel, 5151 Pooks Hill Road, Bethesda, MD 20814; (301) 897–9400 or (800) 228–9290; fax (301) 897–4156.
♦ Holiday Inn Select Bethesda, 8120 Wisconsin Avenue, Bethesda, MD 20814; (301) 652–2000 or (800) HOLIDAY; fax (301) 652–4525.

BIKE SHOPS

♦ Revolution Cycles, at the foot of Key Bridge, 3411 M Street N.W., Washington, D.C. 20007; (202) 965–3601.
♦ The Bicycle Pro Shop, 3403 M Street N.W., Washington, D.C. 20007; (202) 337–0311.

MAPS

♦ ADC's *Washington Area Bike Map*. Compiled by Metropolitan Washington Council of Governments. $10.95. Available at bookstores and newsstands.
♦ *D.C. Bikeways*. Series of maps published by the city. $3.00. Write to District of Columbia Office of Documents, 441 Fourth Street N.W., Suite 520, Washington, D.C. 20001; (202) 727–5090.
♦ *Maryland Bicycle Touring Map*. Free. Available from Office of Tourism Development, 45 Calvert Street, Annapolis, MD 21401.
♦ *Trails in Montgomery County Parks*. Contact Maryland National Capital Parks and Planning Commission (MNCPPC), 8787 Georgia Avenue N.W., Silver Spring, MD 20910; (301) 495–2503; www.mncppc.org.

Capital Crescent Ramble

T his is a weekend favorite of many riders in the D.C. area, who know it as the "Yuri Ride"—named for a Guatemalan with a Russian cosmonaut's moniker. Every Sunday for years, Yuri led a procession of bikes along this route. He led them on in-line skates, and they had to work to keep up! It now includes quaint riverside trails in addition to a scenic tour of Bethesda, Rock Creek Park, and Georgetown.

Over the past decade or so, hundreds of communities across the country have turned abandoned railroad rights-of-way into attractive multiuse trails and linear parks. These "rail-to-trail" conversions have proved hugely popular. Their gentle grade makes them ideal for walking, jogging, in-line skating, cycling, and more.

At last count there were nearly 1,000 completed rail-trails, totaling more than 10,000 miles, in every state of the Union as well as Washington, D.C. They range in length from a few miles to a few hundred miles.

The Washington area joined the movement in a big way in the 1980s with the completion of the 45-mile-long W & OD Trail from Arlington to the town of Purcellville, in the shadow of the Blue Ridge Mountains (see this book's next ride for complete details). Then came the 12-mile WB & A Trail in Prince George's and Anne Arundel Counties.

Now, with the completion of its initial 7-mile stretch from the heart of Georgetown to downtown Bethesda, the Capital Crescent Trail joins the list. Although relatively short, it boasts Potomac River views, a restored trestle bridge over the C & O Canal, and a brick-vaulted railroad tunnel. It also offers a completely car-free commuting route from Bethesda to downtown. And for longer rides it features direct connections to the C & O towpath (Ride 14), Rock Creek Park (Ride 4), and Virginia's extensive trail system (Rides 1, 15, and 16).

A curve on the C & O Canal

This ride connects the paved Capital Crescent Trail, the gravel Georgetown Branch Trail, and Rock Creek Park. The resulting loop is high on fun, short on cars, and lacking in noticeable hills. The full loop is best on weekends when Beach Drive in Rock Creek Park is closed to traffic.

Start in downtown Bethesda, at the corner of Woodmont and Bethesda Avenues. Look for the entrance to the Capital Crescent Trail between the public parking lot on the corner and the car dealership on Bethesda Avenue. A natural food market, two bagel stores, and a gourmet coffee shop—all within yards of the trailhead—offer an opportunity to fuel up for your ride. In the spirit of saving the best for last, though, ride away from the trail, following Bethesda Avenue to a tunnel under Wisconsin Avenue and onto the Georgetown Branch Trail.

The Georgetown Branch Trail winds through Chevy Chase, one of Washington's classic old neighborhoods. After passing older bungalows and colonial-style homes, you'll ride through the Chevy Chase Country Club. Proper etiquette demands that everyone—including riders—be quiet when golfers are putting.

For now, the Georgetown Branch Trail is hard-packed gravel. This bike path is planned to become part of the paved Capital Crescent Trail linking Georgetown with Silver Spring, Maryland. Follow the Georgetown Branch Trail until it intersects with the Rock Creek Trail, then take that trail back into downtown Washington. (See Ride 3 for complete details on this stretch.)

THE BASICS

Start: Public parking lot on the corner of Bethesda and Woodmont Avenues in Bethesda

Distance: 22 miles

Approximate pedaling time: 3 hours

Terrain and surface: Flat; paved recreational trails and gravel bike paths

Things to see: Area's newest rail-to-trail conversion project, the C & O Canal, a bit of downtown Bethesda, old Chevy Chase houses, Rock Creek Park

Traffic and hazards: Mostly bike paths, no cars. Some gravel trail sections.

Facilities: Restrooms at Fletcher's Boat House; food available anywhere in Bethesda.

Getting there: Start at the public parking lot at the corner of Bethesda and Woodmont Avenues in Bethesda. From downtown D.C., follow Wisconsin Avenue to Bethesda, then turn left onto Leland Street to Woodmont and Bethesda Avenues. From the direction of Rockville, follow Wisconsin Avenue into town, then turn right onto Woodmont just past the National Institutes of Health and continue to Bethesda Avenue. Or take the Metro to the Bethesda station on the Red Line. Exit via the Metro elevator onto Wisconsin Avenue, follow Wisconsin Avenue south for 3 blocks to Bethesda Avenue, then turn right for 2 blocks to Woodmont.

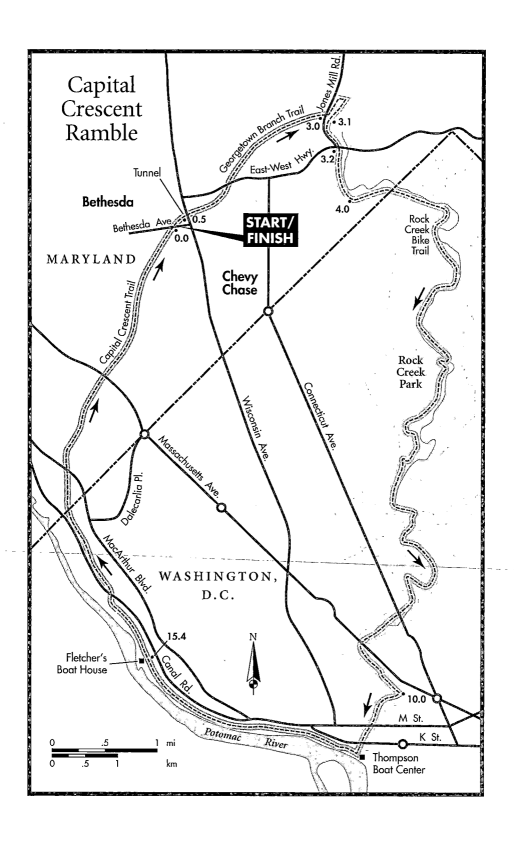

Capital
Crescent
Ramble

Bethesda

MARYLAND

Tunnel

Bethesda Ave. 0.5

0.0

Georgetown Branch Trail

Jones Mill Rd.

3.0 •3.1

East-West Hwy. 3.2

4.0

START/
FINISH

**Chevy
Chase**

Capital Crescent Trail

Rock
Creek
Bike
Trail

Rock
Creek
Park

Wisconsin Ave.

Connecticut Ave.

Massachusetts Ave.

Dalecarlia Pl.

MacArthur Blvd.

WASHINGTON,
D.C.

N

15.4

Fletcher's
Boat House

Canal Rd.

10.0

M St.

K St.

Potomac   River

Thompson
Boat Center

0   .5   1   mi

0   .5   1   km

0.0 From the entrance to the Capital Crescent Trail on Bethesda Avenue, turn right and cross Woodmont Avenue.

0.5 Turn left onto the bike path leading to a tunnel under Wisconsin Avenue. At the end of the tunnel, hard-packed gravel marks the start of the Georgetown Branch Trail. Follow the trail past the golf course. Cross Connecticut Avenue and ride on the sidewalk to reach the bike trail.

3.0 Cross Jones Bridge Road, then make a quick left and right onto Susanna Lane. Follow the road around to the left and back onto the bike path.

3.1 Shortly, the Georgetown Branch Trail will intersect with the Rock Creek Trail. Turn right onto the Rock Creek Trail, toward downtown Washington, D.C.

3.2 Continue straight on the Rock Creek Trail where the Georgetown Branch Trail goes off to the left at a small playground.

3.5 Cross East-West Highway onto Meadowbrook Lane. Keeping the stables on your right, turn right toward Meadowbrook Park.

4.0 At the park, turn right over a small bridge, then left onto Beach Drive. Follow the Rock Creek bike path toward Georgetown. (See Ride 3 for details.)

10.0 Pass under M Street and Pennsylvania Avenue overpasses. Fifty yards after riding beneath overpasses, turn right onto a brick path leading into the C & O Canal National Historic Park. Follow it 2 blocks and turn left onto Thirtieth Street. You've missed it if you reach Thompson Boat Center in another 100 yards. Turn right onto K Street under the Whitehurst Freeway. Ride the full length of K Street to the beginning of the Capital Crescent Trail. Follow the Capital Crescent Trail for its entire length back to Bethesda. Along the way, you'll ride alongside the C & O Canal before crossing a bridge over it; pass through a tunnel beneath MacArthur Boulevard; cross a bridge over Massachusetts Avenue; and cross Little Falls Parkway.

22.0 Reach the trail's end at Bethesda Avenue.

Now comes the only tricky part. Just after crossing beneath the M Street and Pennsylvania Avenue overpasses, turn right onto the brick path leading into the C & O Canal National Historic Park. (You've gone too far if you reach Thompson Boat House on the right in another 100 yards.) Ride along the canal for 2 blocks, then turn left onto Thirtieth Street down to K Street, which runs under the Whitehurst Freeway. Turn right onto K Street, and ride the length of K Street, passing the Washington Harbor development and the rest of Georgetown's waterfront on the left. At the very end, where K Street ends, the Capital Crescent Trail begins.

This trail (paved in 1995) traces the east bank of the Potomac River for a few miles before turning inland toward Bethesda. The views are best in fall or early spring, before thick growth turns it into a tunnel of greenery. You'll ride alongside the C & O Canal towpath for a short stretch. Fletcher's Boat House is on the left, where you can rent rowboats and one-speed bicycles (202–244–0461). The trail then curves right, crossing a restored railroad trestle bridge over the canal. Be sure to rest here for the view.

The trail's approximate midway point is marked by a cavernous, brick-vaulted tunnel beneath MacArthur Boulevard. The Bethesda public swimming pool at Little Falls Road will seem particularly welcoming on a hot summer day. (Be sure to pack a bathing suit, towel, and about $10 per person for snacks and entrance fees.) From there, it's just another 0.5 mile to the trail's end at Bethesda Avenue.

LOCAL INFORMATION

♦ D.C. Chamber of Commerce, 1213 K Street N.W., Washington, D.C. 20005; (202) 347–7201.
♦ Conference and Visitors Bureau of Montgomery County, MD, Inc., 11820 Parklawn Drive, Suite 380, Rockville, MD 20852; (301) 428–9702 or (800) 925–0880.
♦ Montgomery County Recreation Department, 12210 Bushey Drive, Silver Spring, MD 20902; (240) 777–6804 (general information—recording).

LOCAL EVENTS/ATTRACTIONS

♦ Rock Creek Park, Washington, D.C.; www.nps.gov. Luckily for Washingtonians, in 1890 Congress prevented this 1,800-acre green valley that cuts a swathe from Georgetown north through the city to the Maryland state line from becoming the unofficial city dump. Today this tranquil urban valley is a haven for bikers, joggers, and picnickers. It is a place where people can enjoy themselves, sitting quietly under the shade trees along the banks of the creek, cooking over a barbecue grill or enjoying the sight and fragrance of the daffodils and other flowers that bloom here each spring.
♦ Rock Creek Park Nature Center & Planetarium, 5200 Glover Road N.W., Washington, D.C.; (202) 426–6829. A spot where you can see live and mounted wildlife displays, environmental exhibits, and planetarium shows, as well as participate in guided nature walks. For horseback-riding lessons, visit the Horse Centre off Military Road at 5100 Glover Road N.W. Call (202) 362–0117.

ACCOMMODATIONS

◆ Bed & Breakfast Accommodations, P.O. Box 12011, Washington, D.C. 20005; (202) 328–3510; www.bnbaccom.com.

◆ Washington D.C. Accommodations, 2201 Wisconsin Avenue, Suite C110, Washington, D.C. 20007; (202) 289–2220 or (800) 554–2220; www.wdcahotels.com.

◆ Bethesda Marriott Hotel, 5151 Pooks Hill Road, Bethesda, MD 20814; (301) 897–9400 or (800) 228–9290; fax (301) 897–4156.

◆ Holiday Inn Select Bethesda, 8120 Wisconsin Avenue, Bethesda, MD 20814; (301) 652–2000 or (800) HOLIDAY; fax (301) 652–4525.

BIKE SHOPS

◆ Revolution Cycles, at the foot of Key Bridge, 3411 M Street N.W., Washington, D.C. 20007; (202) 965–3601.

◆ The Bicycle Pro Shop, 3403 M Street N.W., Washington, D.C. 20007; (202) 337–0311.

◆ Big Wheel Bikes, 1034 Thirty-third Street N.W., Washington, D.C.; (202) 337–0254.

◆ Big Wheel Bikes, 6917 Arlington Road, Bethesda, MD 20814; (301) 652–0192.

MAPS

◆ *ADC's Washington Area Bike Map.* Compiled by Metropolitan Washington Council of Governments. $10.95. Available at bookstores and newsstands.

◆ *D.C. Bikeways.* Series of maps published by the city. $3.00. Write to District of Columbia Office of Documents, 441 Fourth Street N.W., Suite 520, Washington, D.C. 20001; (202) 727–5090.

◆ *Maryland Bicycle Touring Map.* Free. Available from Office of Tourism Development, 45 Calvert Street, Annapolis, MD 21401.

◆ *Trails in Montgomery County Parks.* Contact Maryland–National Capital Park and Planning Commission (MNCPPC), 8787 Georgia Avenue N.W., Silver Spring, MD 20910; (301) 495–2503; www.mncppc.org.

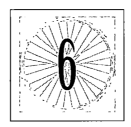

W & OD Trail Cruise

THROUGH VIRGINIA COUNTRYSIDE

*I**f you've ever wanted to just get out in the sunshine and ride—this is the trail for you! It's paved and only mildly hilly. Most of all, it's gorgeous riding surrounded by cheerful, helpful folks. Ten miles into the trail, there's a rest stop fully stocked with vending machines and picnic tables. But don't let that fool you—this drag is also used by serious riders to train twice a week. You'll be amazed at how close to D.C. you can find far-stretching farm fields.*

The Washington & Old Dominion Railroad never was very successful. Founded in 1847 to connect towns on the Potomac to resort towns in the Blue Ridge Mountains, the rail line that locals dubbed the "Virginia Creeper" ran sporadically and lost money for more than a century until closing for good in 1968.

Today, however, the W & OD line is a stunning success. Its 100-foot-wide right-of-way has been converted to a park stretching from the Arlington/ Alexandria border to the rural town of Purcellville, 45 miles away. The Northern Virginia Regional Park Authority has created one of the most convenient, safe, and interesting trails in the capital region. You can easily reach the W & OD by Metrorail, superhighway, or other off-road trails (see Ride 15 for a connecting route). From Vienna to Purcellville, the wide, paved trail is augmented by a separate 30-mile gravel bridle path. The park authority constructed or restored seventeen bridges to whisk cyclists over streambeds and busy roads.

Dozens of roads and parking lots connect to the W & OD, so you can pick a starting point at will. One of the most popular is the Metrorail station in East

Falls Church, from where you will encounter only a few miles of suburbia before getting to the "good stuff." Falls Church and Vienna, the next town along the trail, have interesting historic areas. In particular, the old train depot in Vienna now houses an elaborate model train operated by the Northern Virginia Model Railroaders Association. Traversing these towns does require some tedious crossings of busy roads and shopping plazas.

For a shorter ride that skips this suburban stretch, begin near the 17-mile marker in the planned community of Reston. Reston was founded in 1963 by Robert E. Simon, who envisioned a utopian community of mixed ages and income levels. Until recently, most of Reston looked like typical suburbia, but the new Reston Town Center has brought some urban splash. Located smack up against the W & OD, the eighty-five-acre area tries to re-create an open-air, lively city neighborhood: brick sidewalks, outdoor cafes, sixty shops of the BenneGapLimited variety, movie theaters, linden trees lined up along the streets, and a European-style central fountain. In keeping with the haute boutique atmosphere, there's a fancy bike shop that features a granite waterfall, polished hardwood floors—and bike rentals. A few miles ahead the old burgs of Herndon and Sterling have retained their neat town centers. Farther west, the cyclist encounters open fields and picturesque streams, beginning with Broad Run.

Crossing Route 7 on the W & OD Trail

THE BASICS

Start: East Falls Church Metro station

Distance: 39 miles, one way

Approximate pedaling time: 4 hours

Terrain and surface: Mostly flat and straight; paved multiuse trail

Things to see: Historic train stations, farms, creeks, downtown Leesburg historic district

Traffic and hazards: You'll cross a number of neighborhood streets initially, but thoroughfares have bridge crossings. The farther out you ride, the fewer road crossings you'll encounter.

Facilities: Rest rooms, restaurants, bike shops, country stores en route

Getting there: By auto, Interstate 66 or 495 to East Falls Church; park at Metro station. By Metro, Orange Line to East Falls Church station. By bike, Interstate 66 bike trail, which stretches from Key Bridge in Rosslyn to merge with W & OD Trail (see description in Ride 15).

The scenery is now divided between broad vistas and low gullies lined by thick underbrush. More than 450 wildflower species grow along the W & OD, including Virginia creeper, a vine with berries and five-pronged leaves. After passing an old quarry, you come to the country town of Ashburn. Be sure to stop at Partlow's Store, where you can buy anything from bananas to wading boots. The friendly dog on the porch *will* try to steal your granola bars.

Ride over an old railroad bridge over Goose Creek, and soon you're on the outskirts of Leesburg, seat of Loudoun County. Turn right onto Catoctin Circle and right again onto Market Street for a look at the old courthouse and the narrow streets of the historic district. The town was first named Georgetown for the king, and renamed in the 1700s for Thomas Lee, a wily planter and trader who excelled at Indian negotiations.

Leesburg was a Civil War site of minor importance. In an effort to dislodge Confederate troops in 1861, Union forces invaded the town via the 100-foot cliffs of Ball's Bluff. They were spectacularly rebuffed and suffered 1,700 casualties. An apocryphal tale has it that corpses of the blue brigade washed up 40 miles downriver in Washington's commercial district.

The W & OD runs another 9 miles west through rolling Loudoun County, ending in the old town of Purcellville. If the park authority reaches its goal of extending the trail a few miles more to Bluemont, they will have effected a connection to the 2,100-mile Appalachian Trail for hiking. In 1987 the U.S. Department of the Interior designated the whole park as a National Recreation Trail.

If you're interested in exploring the W & OD thoroughly, look for the fifty-six-page *W & OD Trail Guide* at local bike shops or Northern Virginia Regional Parks offices. Or call the W & OD Trail office at (703) 729–0596 to order a copy. For a really long ride, this route connects with Rides 26 and 31.

Recumbents cruising through the woods

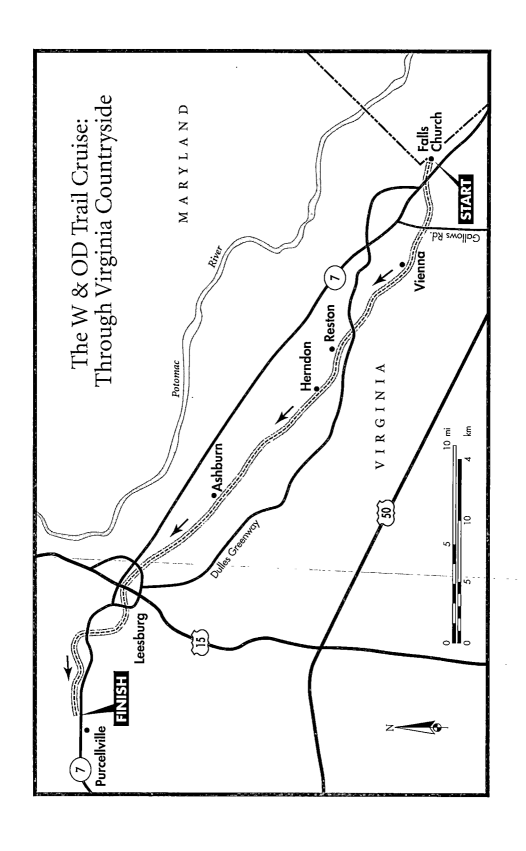

The W & OD Trail Cruise: Through Virginia Countryside

MARYLAND

VIRGINIA

Potomac River

Falls Church

START

Gallows Rd

Vienna

7

Reston

Herndon

Ashburn

Dulles Greenway

50

15

Leesburg

FINISH

Purcellville

7

N

0   5   10 mi

0   5   10   km

0.0 From East Falls Church Metrorail station, turn right on Sycamore Street.
0.1 Turn right onto W. & OD Trail to head toward Purcellville. Trail is well marked.
39.0 Turn left onto W & OD Trail to head toward Arlington. Trail is well marked.

LOCAL INFORMATION

♦ Arlington Chamber of Commerce, 2009 Fourteenth Street, North, Suite 111, Arlington, VA 22201; (703) 525–2400.
♦ Arlington Convention and Visitors Service, 1100 North Glebe Road, Suite 1500, Arlington, VA 22201; (703) 228–0888 or (800) 677–6267.
♦ Loudon Convention and Visitors Association, 108-D South Street, Leesburg, VA 20175; (800) 752–6118.

LOCAL EVENTS/ATTRACTIONS

♦ Annual Waterford Homes Tour and Crafts Exhibit, first weekend in October; (540) 882–3085.

RESTAURANTS

♦ Lost Dog Cafe, Westover Shopping Center, 5876 North Washington Boulevard, Arlington, VA 22205; (703) 237–1552. Probably the best place in town.
♦ Candelora's at the Purcellville Inn, 36855 West Main Street, Purcellville, VA 20132; (540) 338–2075. An Italian restaurant in a restored inn.

ACCOMMODATIONS

♦ Best Western Key Bridge, 1850 North Fort Myer Drive, Arlington, VA 22209; (703) 522–0400 or (800) KEY–BRIDGE.
♦ Georges Mill Farm B&B, 11867 Georges Mill Road, Lovettsville, VA 20180; (540) 822–5224.

BIKE SHOPS

♦ Revolution Cycles, 2731 Wilson Boulevard, Arlington, VA 22201; (703) 312–0007.
♦ Trailside Bicycles, 201 North Twenty-first Street, Purcellville, VA 20132; (540) 338–4687.

♦ *W & OD R.R. Regional Park Trail Guide.* $5.95. Contact Northern Virginia Regional Park Authority, 5400 Ox Road, Fairfax Station, VA 22039; (703) 352–5900. Also available from the W & OD Trail office at (703) 729–0596 and some bike shops.

♦ *Arlington, Virginia, Bikeway Map and Guide.* Published by the Arlington County Department of Public Works. Free. Contact Public Works Planning Division, No. 1 Court House Plaza, 2100 North Clarendon Boulevard, Arlington, VA 22201; (703) 228–3681.

♦ *Virginia Atlas· and Gazetteer.* Published by DeLorme Mapping Company. Includes topographic maps, hike/bike trails, canoeing area. $12.95. Available at bookstores.

♦ *ADC's Washington Area Bike Map.* Compiled by Metropolitan Washington Council of Governments. $10.95. Available at bookstores and newsstands.

♦ *D.C. Bikeways.* Series of maps published by the city. $3.00. Write to District of Columbia Office of Documents, 441 Fourth Street N.W., Suite 520, Washington, D.C. 20001; (202) 727–5090.

Mount Vernon Trail Ramble

TO OLD TOWN ALEXANDRIA

O n Sunday mornings I often slip away to points usually too crowded to enjoy intimately. My avenue for this furtive endeavor is the Mount Vernon Trail, an 18.5-mile off-road path that links Washington with the estate of the president for whom the city was named. In between lies historic Alexandria, Virginia, a minor port in colonial America and a major tourist attraction today.

The trail parallels the George Washington Memorial Parkway, a scenic road built in 1932 for the bicentennial of the first president's birth. This ride begins at Harry T. Thompson Boat Center in Washington. (Turn to the end of this chapter for an alternative starting point at Theodore Roosevelt Island on the Virginia side.) Leaving Thompson's, turn right onto a path. As described in Ride 1, proceed to the Jefferson Memorial and cross the Fourteenth Street Bridge bike path to Virginia. At the end of the bridge, bear right onto a short stretch of path that drops down to river level. Turn right onto the Mount Vernon Trail, heading downriver.

Passing a soccer field on the right, come to Gravelly Point, a good place to see the monuments—and landing jets—in profile. Continue through a parking lot to traverse Reagan National Airport. This part isn't the most scenic ride in the world, but it's not without interest. Much of the 750-acre airport was built in the 1930s under WPA programs, and the original buildings retain some of their streamlined, New Deal charm. In 1997 a mammoth new main terminal was dedicated. In 1998, on the eve of his eighty-seventh birthday, the airport was named for former president Ronald Reagan. Carefully cross four parkway ramps to reach the marina at Daingerfield Island. On any given day this

Start: Thompson Boat Center

Distance: 22-mile loop

Approximate pedaling time: 2–3 hours

Terrain and surface: Flat; smooth off-road trails and some busy roads

Things to see: Jefferson Memorial, Reagan National Airport, sailing marina, historic Alexandria, Hunting Creek wildlife area

Traffic and hazards: Use caution at busy traffic crossings at beginning and end of ride. The remainder of the ride is a well-kept, safe-from-traffic bike path. It's best to dismount and walk under the overpasses, as the sidewalks are a tight fit.

Facilities: Rest rooms, snack bar, and bike shop at Daingerfield Island Marina

Getting there: From north, Rock Creek Parkway to Thompson's parking lot; turn right. From Mall, Virginia Avenue west across Rock Creek Parkway to Thompson's parking lot. From Virginia, Roosevelt Bridge or Memorial Bridge to Rock Creek Parkway to Thompson's. By Metro, Blue or Orange Line to Foggy Bottom/GWU, about a 1-mile walk or ride. From Metro station, walk south on Twenty-third Street (away from Washington Circle). Turn right onto H Street; left onto New Hampshire Avenue, and right on Virginia Avenue. Cross Rock Creek Parkway at crosswalk to reach parking lot of Thompson Boat Center. Follow one-lane road over short bridge to waterfront.

windswept spit attracts hundreds of sailors, sunbathers, and sailboarders. You will also find a snack bar, bike shop, restaurant, and rest rooms. Bike and boat rentals are available at the marina. For information call (703) 548–9027.

Now head south through a marsh full of cattails. Keep an eye out for circling hawks. When the path comes to a fork, bear left for a ride *above* the Potomac. To get around the area's industrial property, the park service built a cantilevered trail protruding from a retaining wall and supported by diagonal steel struts. The scenery is now a mixture of new office parks, an old rail line, Potomac vistas, and Alexandria's network of waterfront parks. Take a short detour through the Canal Square office complex to view a most unusual fountain. After crossing the railroad bed, graded flush with the road, reach North Union Street, heading for Alexandria's historic heart.

Founded by Scottish immigrants and laid out in 1749 with help from surveyor George Washington, Alexandria grew into a thriving tobacco port. In 1791 the burg was incorporated into the nascent District of Columbia. Town leaders agitated successfully for a return to mother Virginia in 1846. Alexandria escaped destruction during the Civil War, thereby retaining a large collection of brick and gingerbread houses of all eras.

It's easy to roam the gridiron of 200 city blocks by bicycle. Particularly worthwhile are Queen and Prince Streets (perpendicular to the river), and Royal and St. Asaph Streets (parallel to the waterfront). The city's housing

Early morning ride down the river

trademark is the oblong "flounder house," whose side porch looks like it should face front. King Street hums with bookshops, pubs, and restaurants. Heading uphill, it leads to the 330-foot-tall George Washington Masonic Memorial, the area's second tallest building after the Washington Monument.

Be sure to visit historic Christ Church, attended by both George Washington and Robert E. Lee; the Lyceum, a history museum; and the Torpedo Factory, a World War I munitions plant that now houses 200 artists' studios. There's a visitor center at 221 King Street.

Back on your two-wheeler, head south on North Union Street. Follow bike-path signs until you reach the end of North Union, where the bike path continues through a wooded area to Jones Point, the site of an old whitewashed lighthouse marking the city's original southern tip. After visiting the lighthouse, retrace your steps and follow the bike-path signs until you reach busy Washington Street. The route continues on a sidewalk. In a few hundred feet, stop at a stone bridge and pull out your lightweight binoculars. Among tidal flats and rotting piers, you can spot snowy egrets, hooded mergansers, and buf-flehead ducks, not to mention eagles and falcons.

Rather than moving on to Mount Vernon—the route there from Alexandria is covered in the next chapter—turn around for a slightly different return to Washington. Follow the alternate bike route on Royal Street, a typical Old Town lane with narrow row houses. Turn left onto King Street to visit the

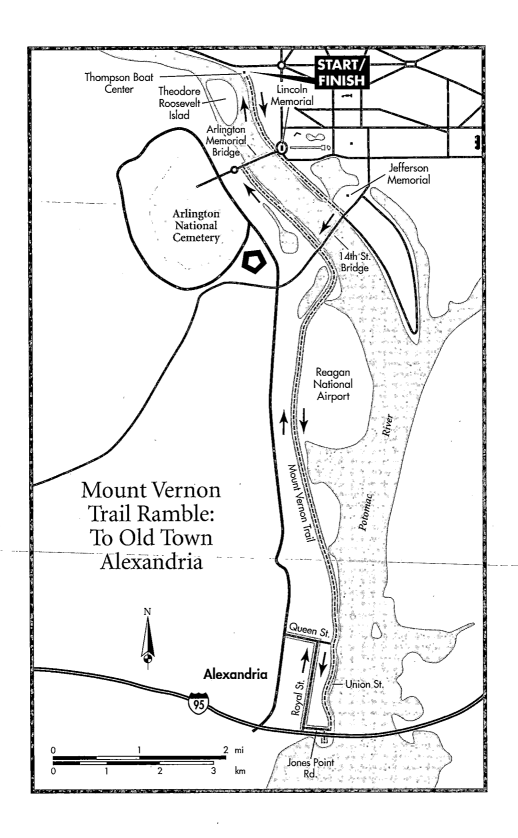

START/FINISH

Thompson Boat Center

Theodore Roosevelt Islad

Lincoln Memorial

Arlington Memorial Bridge

Jefferson Memorial

Arlington National Cemetery

14th St. Bridge

Reagan National Airport

River

Mount Vernon Trail

Potomac

Mount Vernon
Trail Ramble:
To Old Town
Alexandria

N

Queen St.

Alexandria

Royal St.

Union St.

95

0   1   2 mi
0   1   2   3 km

Jones Point Rd.

Note: Use blocks and features instead of miles for navigation.

♦ From Thompson Boat Center, right on bike path toward Watergate Apartments and Kennedy Center, Potomac River on right.

♦ Cross parkway intersection to reach path continuing between volleyball courts.

♦ Ride or walk through two short bridge underpasses.

♦ Straight through traffic circle at Ericsson Monument to Ohio Drive.

♦ Straight on Ohio Drive past soccer fields to cross 1909 bridge. Left at circular garden.

♦ Across from Jefferson Memorial entrance, right at curb cut to reach bikeway over Fourteenth Street Bridge.

♦ Cross bridge and bear right on bike path down to river level. Turn right onto Mount Vernon Trail, heading downriver.

♦ Follow trail signs past Reagan National Airport and sailing marina.

♦ In 4 miles, cross railroad tracks. Trail continues on North Union Street in Old Town Alexandria.

♦ Follow North Union to end of street onto off-road bike path. Path rejoins Jones Point Road parallel to Interstate 95.

♦ Turn left to visit historic Jones Point lighthouse. Retrace route and continue on Jones Point Road.

♦ Follow on-road path to Hunting Towers apartment complex at Washington Street. Left on sidewalk.

♦ Turn around at Hunting Creek Bridge. Retrace steps; bear left on Royal Street, on-road bike route through upper Old Town.

♦ Right onto Queen Street. Left onto Union to rejoin Mount Vernon route.

♦ Straight on Mount Vernon Trail past Navy and Marine Memorial and Lady Bird Johnson Park.

♦ To reach Memorial Bridge, bear left at fork in trail and cross George Washington Parkway three times at crosswalks marked with stripes.

♦ Using Memorial Bridge sidewalk, cross to D.C. to Lincoln Memorial.

♦ Take unmarked path back to Ericsson Monument and retrace path to Thompson's.

Masonic Memorial, or catch Metrorail's Yellow Line back to downtown D.C. Otherwise, head north to Queen Street, turn right, and rejoin the bike path at Founders Park on the waterfront.

In 4 miles bypass the Fourteenth Street Bridge and keep straight. Pass the Lady Bird Johnson Park and bear left where the path continues under Memorial Bridge. Cross the George Washington Parkway and follow the bike path over three roads and onto the sidewalk of Memorial Bridge. Off to the left

Buildings on this ride take us back to when Alexandria was a tobacco port.

you can see eighty-eight-acre Theodore Roosevelt Island, once a country estate and now a park. Follow the bike route past the Lincoln Memorial and back to Thompson's.

Option: To shorten this ride and skip its two crossings over the Potomac River, start at Theodore Roosevelt Island on the Virginia side. Park in the lot just off the George Washington Memorial Parkway. Ride south on the new boardwalk/asphalt path to connect with the Mount Vernon Trail. When you return, take the time to explore at least some of the island's 2.5 miles of trails and its memorial plaza.

LOCAL INFORMATION

♦ Alexandria Chamber of Commerce, 801 North Fairfax Street, Suite 402, Alexandria, VA 22314; (703) 549–1000.
♦ Ramsay House Visitors Center, 221 King Street, Alexandria, VA 22314; (703) 838–4200 or (800) 388–9119. Open daily from 9:00 A.M. to 5:00 P.M. Closed Thanksgiving, Christmas, and New Year's. Located in Old Town Alexandria and staffed by knowledgeable travel counselors, this visitor center is a great resource for detailed information about attractions, tours, accommodations, dining, shopping, special events, and more. Brochures and maps are available.
♦ Alexandria Convention & Visitors Association, 421 King Street, Suite 300, Alexandria, VA 22314; (703) 838–4200 or (800) 388–9119; ACVA@FunSide.com.

LOCAL EVENTS/ATTRACTIONS

♦ Historic Alexandria has events and attractions occurring year-round. Contact the chamber of commerce with the time of your visit for a detailed list.

ACCOMMODATIONS

♦ Alexandria Hotel Association Accommodation, (800) 296–1000. This organization will check availability and rates, and make reservations at hotels.

BIKE SHOPS

♦ Revolution Cycles, at the foot of Key Bridge, 3411 M Street N.W., Washington, D.C.; (202) 965–3601.
♦ The Bicycle Pro Shop, 3403 M Street N.W., Washington, D.C. 20007; (202) 337–0311.
♦ Big Wheel Bikes, 1034 Thirty-third Street N.W., Washington, D.C. 20007; (202) 337–0254.
♦ Big Wheel Bikes, 2 Prince Street, Alexandria, VA 22314; (703) 739–2300.
♦ Also at Daingerfield Island Marina.

MAPS

♦ *Arlington, Virginia, Bikeway Map and Guide.* Published by the Arlington County Department of Public Works. Free. Contact Public Works Planning Division, No. 1 Court House Plaza, 2100 North Clarendon Boulevard, Arlington, VA 22201; (703) 228–3681.

♦ *Virginia Atlas and Gazetteer.* Published by DeLorme Mapping Company. Includes topographic maps, hike/bike trails, canoeing areas. $12.95. Available at bookstores.

♦ *ADC's Washington Area Bike Map.* Compiled by Metropolitan Washington Council of Governments. $10.95. Available at bookstores and newsstands.

♦ *D.C. Bikeways.* Series of maps published by the city. $3.00. Write to District of Columbia Office of Documents, 441 Fourth Street N.W., Suite 520, Washington, D.C. 20001; (202) 727–5090.

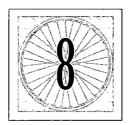

Mount Vernon Trail Ramble

ALEXANDRIA TO MOUNT VERNON

*A*lexandria is an explosion for the senses with its cacophony of sounds and stimulating sights. The timeless buildings and chatter of tourists contrast starkly to the tranquility and natural surroundings of the route to Mount Vernon. This half of the Mount Vernon Trail will reward you with a rich visual experience, and the hills will provide you an exhilarating workout.

———————————————————

The final 8-mile leg of the Mount Vernon Trail resembles a trip to a country estate. It is far more bucolic than the first section. The terrain is also more undulating, which provides some Potomac views.

Start in Old Town Alexandria at the King Street Metrorail station. You can either arrive by Metro or park at the station. Head away from the station on King Street, which is lined with antiques stores and pubs. In 1 mile turn right onto Union Street to join the Mount Vernon Trail.

As described in Ride 7, follow signs to Hunting Creek, then continue straight, with a marshy area of the Potomac due left. You will soon arrive at two parks. The first, Belle Haven, indeed provides respite for sailors, picnickers, and bird-watchers. In season you can rent small sailboats here. Next door stands Dyke Marsh, a 240-acre wildlife preserve rescued from an earlier life as a gravel pit. If it's not muddy, ride out on a spit that juts into the Potomac for a look at this sprawling cattail marsh. In spring the sanctuary hosts 250 bird species, not to mention wild irises, muskrats, frogs, and turtles. It's a glimpse of what these banks looked like two centuries ago.

Back on the route to Mount Vernon, the trail continues on a boardwalk through the marsh. There's a bench for pausing and pondering. Last time there

Start: King Street Metrorail station

Distance: 18-mile loop

Approximate pedaling time: 2 hours

Terrain and surface: Rolling; smooth off-road trails and boardwalks

Things to see: Old Town Alexandria, Dyke Marsh, Fort Hunt Park, Riverside Park, Mount Vernon

Traffic and hazards: None

Facilities: Rest rooms at parks, food and souvenirs at Mount Vernon

Options: 6-mile trip to Woodlawn Plantation; Fort Hunt Park

Getting there: By Metro, Yellow Line to King Street in Alexandria. By car, George Washington Memorial Parkway south to Washington Street; turn right onto King Street and drive 1 mile to Metro parking lot, or continue straight 3 miles to Belle Haven/Dyke Marsh parking area. By bike, combine with route described in Ride 7.

I was treated to a five-minute dogfight as a fish hawk, its talons flaring, buzzed any herons and hawks that dared enter its territory.

Soon the path becomes more winding as hardwood forest closes in. After crossing a bridge across the parkway—noting the handsome construction of the stone span—glide downhill on a grassy median planted with blooming trees and evergreens, then climb again up to a bluff with fine views. The stone structure across the river is Fort Washington, a star-shaped fortress designed by Washington planner Pierre L'Enfant. Coast down to Fort Hunt Park, which has its own military ruins among 156 acres of picnic grounds.

Other sites worth visiting along the path include River Farm, a former holding of George Washington that is now the headquarters of the American Horticultural Society (the public is welcome to tour the gardens and picnic on the river), and Riverside Park, a picnic area on a mini spit of land next to Little Hunting Creek, just before the approach to Mount Vernon.

The remainder of the trail stays close to inlets and bays of the river until it jinks to the right and then climbs, signaling the approach to the estate of George and Martha Washington. Located on high ground on a bend in the river, the crescent-shaped house is surprisingly small but faultlessly elegant. Its Georgian facade was designed to fool the eye. It resembles sandstone but, when tapped, resounds with a knock. To simulate more expensive material, the colonials molded wood into masonrylike blocks and mixed sand with the paint for a rough finish.

The grounds also feature winding paths, formal gardens, trees planted by the general himself, and outbuildings filled with colonial tools and carriages. The estate is lovingly maintained and interpreted by the Mount Vernon Ladies' Association, which also provides tours. In 1858 the group rescued Mount Vernon from ruin, thereby launching the American historic preservation movement—and making possible the survival of many other sites noted in this book.

Leaving Mount Vernon, carefully cross a traffic circle for an optional 6-mile round trip to another site associated with Washington. The Mount Vernon Highway leads to Woodlawn Plantation, once home to Washington's adopted daughter, Nelly Custis Lewis. It's now a house museum run by the National Trust for Historic Preservation. Here the Garden Club of Virginia carefully tends thirty-six rose beds hedged by dwarf species of English boxwood. Also on the grounds is a Frank Lloyd Wright house, which the National Trust rescued from a highway's path and moved to Woodlawn in the 1950s.

LOCAL INFORMATION

♦ Alexandria Chamber of Commerce, 801 North Fairfax Street, Suite 402, Alexandria, VA 22314; (703) 549–1000.
♦ Ramsay House Visitors Center, 221 King Street, Alexandria, VA 22314; (703) 838–4200 or (800) 388–9119. Open daily from 9:00 A.M. to 5:00 P.M. Closed Thanksgiving, Christmas, and New Year's. Located in Old Town Alexandria and staffed by knowledgeable travel counselors, the visitor center is a great resource for detailed information about attractions, tours, accommodations, dining, shopping, special events, and more. Brochures and maps available.

Safe idyllic trails

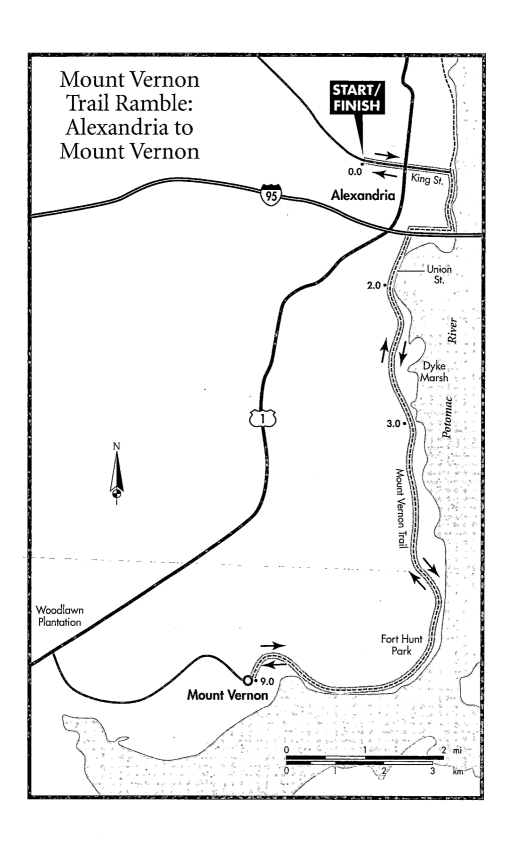

Mount Vernon
Trail Ramble:
Alexandria to
Mount Vernon

START/
FINISH

0.0

King St.

95

Alexandria

Union
St.

2.0

River

Dyke
Marsh

Potomac

3.0

1

N

Mount Vernon Trail

Woodlawn
Plantation

Fort Hunt
Park

9.0

Mount Vernon

0   1   2 mi
0   1   2   3 km

0.0 Start in Alexandria at King Street Metro or Belle Haven picnic area (the latter cuts about 3 miles from trip).

1.0 From King Street, ride east 1 mile to Union Street. Turn right.

2.0 Follow bike-path signs to Hunting Towers apartments on Washington Street. Bear left on sidewalk, which turns into bike path again shortly.

3.0 Follow bike-path signs to Mount Vernon, with optional side trips to Dyke Marsh (1-mile round trip on dirt path) and Fort Hunt Park (1-mile loop on park road).

9.0 Retrace path to starting point.

Option: At Mount Vernon, ride around traffic circle and head west on Mount Vernon Highway. Off-road bike path is available, but on-road shoulder is fairly wide and flat. In 3 miles carefully cross Route 1 to enter Woodlawn Plantation.

♦ Alexandria Convention & Visitors Association, 421 King Street, Suite 300, Alexandria, VA 22314; (703) 838–4200 or (800) 388–9119; ACVA@FunSide.com.

LOCAL EVENTS/ATTRACTIONS

♦ Historic Alexandria has events and attractions occurring year-round. Contact the chamber of commerce with the time of your visit for a detailed list.

ACCOMMODATIONS

♦ Alexandria Hotel Association Accommodation, (800) 296–1000. This organization will check availability and rates, and make reservations at hotels.

BIKE SHOPS

♦ Revolution Cycles, at the foot of Key Bridge, 3411 M Street N.W., Washington, D.C. 20007; (202) 965–3601.

♦ The Bicycle Pro Shop, 3403 M Street N.W., Washington, D.C. 20007; (202) 337–0311.

♦ Big Wheel Bikes, 1034 Thirty-third Street N.W., Washington, D.C. 20007; (202) 337–0254.

♦ Big Wheel Bikes, 2 Prince Street, Alexandria, VA 22314; (703) 739–2300.

♦ Also at Daingerfield Island Marina.

MAPS

♦ *Arlington, Virginia, Bikeway Map and Guide.* Published by the Arlington County Department of Public Works. Free. Contact Public Works Planning

Division, No. 1 Court House Plaza, 2100 North Clarendon Boulevard, Arlington, VA 22201; (703) 228–3681.

♦ *Virginia Atlas and Gazetteer.* Published by DeLorme Mapping Company. Includes topographic maps, hike/bike trails, canoeing areas. $12.95. Available at bookstores.

♦ *ADC's Washington Area Bike Map.* Compiled by Metropolitan Washington Council of Governments. $10.95. Available at bookstores and newsstands.

♦ *D.C. Bikeways.* Series of maps published by the city. $3.00. Write to District of Columbia Office of Documents, 441 Fourth Street N.W., Suite 520, Washington, D.C. 20001; (202) 727–5090.

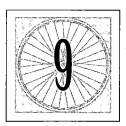

Rosemont Ramble

T his is a sight-seeing figure eight of Alexandria that shows off both
eighteenth-century Old Town and late-nineteenth-century historic neighborhoods. It is easily reached by Metro or bike paths from D.C.

Start at the King Street Metrorail station about 1 mile west of the Potomac
River. The main landmark is a big one: the 330-foot-tall, gray pyramidal tower
of the George Washington Masonic Memorial, built in the early twentieth century with $5 million donated by 3 million members of the Masonic order. It's
the region's tallest structure after the Washington Monument (and, like the big
white needle, it's open to the public, with an elevator ride to the top). Pause en
route to see things like the dioramas depicting Masonic deeds and the trowel
George Washington used to lay the U.S. Capitol's cornerstone. Just south of the
temple is Alexandria Union Station, much less grand than D.C.'s Union Station,
but a quaint stop on Amtrak's southern route nonetheless.

Leave the Metro station and head north under the railroad tracks on King
Street. Take the second right onto Russell Road. You are entering Rosemont, a
pre–World War I suburb that the city of Alexandria annexed in 1915.
Rosemont's raison d'être was the Washington, Alexandria, & Mt. Vernon elec-
tric streetcar line, which brought downtown D.C. within a nickel and eighteen
minutes. (A 1909 ad promised free streetcar tickets to come view model homes
priced from $750 to $1,200.) The streetcar faded away in the 1930s, but Rosemont continued to thrive and today is a well-preserved neighborhood with
neat bungalows mixed in among grander houses with wraparound porches.

Russell Road whisks you through Rosemont before you start climbing the
North Ridge. Located in a small traffic triangle, a cannon mounted on cobblestones and concrete marks the spot where General Edward Braddock led his
troops off in 1755 to defend the western front against the French and their
Indian allies. Stop at Alexandria Country Day School at the top of the hill on

Well-maintained trails can be found all over Virginia.

the left for an excellent view over the Potomac to Maryland. Also known as Shuter's Hill, the ridge was seized by Union troops during the Civil War and laid bare so lookouts would have clear sightlines.

Rosemont segues into Del Ray, a blue-collar neighborhood built to house railroad workers for nearby Potomac Yards. (Del Ray was formerly called Potomac, but its cottages would never be confused with the plummy manses across the river in Potomac, Maryland.) The 320-acre freight yards are giving way to a massive new development called Potomac 2020. After heading downhill, double back through Rosemont along commercial Mount Vernon Avenue. Bear right onto bike-laned Commonwealth Avenue, where the trolley formerly ran on the median strip.

After again threading under the Metrorail tracks and turning left onto Daingerfield Road, head east on Prince Street toward the river. The vacant traffic triangle you pass while making the turn is the former site of Hooff's Run, a creek now channeled through underground pipes.

Alexandria was intended to be a grand and great city until it was outstripped as a port, and its early architecture reflects it. Prince Street is one of Old Town's oldest and most intact thoroughfares. A series of row houses in the 200 block, Gentry Row, dates from 1752 to 1795; 200 Prince belonged to Robert Townshend Hooe, the city's first elected mayor. Another house belonged to Dr. James Craik, the physician at George Washington's side when he died; Craik's colleague and neighbor Dr. Elisha Cullen Dick cut the pendulum cords on the first president's clock to record the time of death. Across the street, the Greek Revival Lyceum, built as a library in 1839, has housed the city's history museum since 1985. At the corner of Prince and busy Washington Streets stands a bronze statue of R. E. Lee Camp, Confederate soldier. The monument offends some, but the Virginia legislature passed a special bill in 1890 ensuring it would never be moved.

Continue down Prince (the last block is cobblestone) to North Union and visit the artsy-craftsy Torpedo Factory (which has a new waterfront "food court," a la shopping malls) before returning to the start via King Street, Old Town's busiest and boutique-iest boulevard. The corner of King and Pitt recorded the Civil War's first casualty: A Union colonel named Ellsworth was shot dead after he tore a Confederate flag from a tavern.

Interestingly, the only marker at this corner is a tribute to James W. Jackson, the First Martyr to the Cause of Southern Independence, who was found by a coroner's inquiry to be defending his property.

LOCAL INFORMATION

♦ Alexandria Chamber of Commerce, 801 North Fairfax Street, Suite 402, Alexandria, VA 22314; (703) 549–1000.

♦ Ramsay House Visitors Center, 221 King Street, Alexandria, VA 22314; (703) 838–4200 or (800) 388–9119. Open daily from 9:00 A.M. to 5:00 P.M. Closed Thanksgiving, Christmas, and New Year's. Located in Old Town Alexandria and staffed by knowledgeable travel counselors, the visitor center is a great resource for detailed information about attractions, tours, accommodations, dining, shopping, special events, and more. Brochures and maps available.

♦ Alexandria Convention & Visitors Association, 421 King Street, Suite 300, Alexandria, VA 22314; (703) 838–4200 or (800) 388–9119; ACVA@FunSide. com.

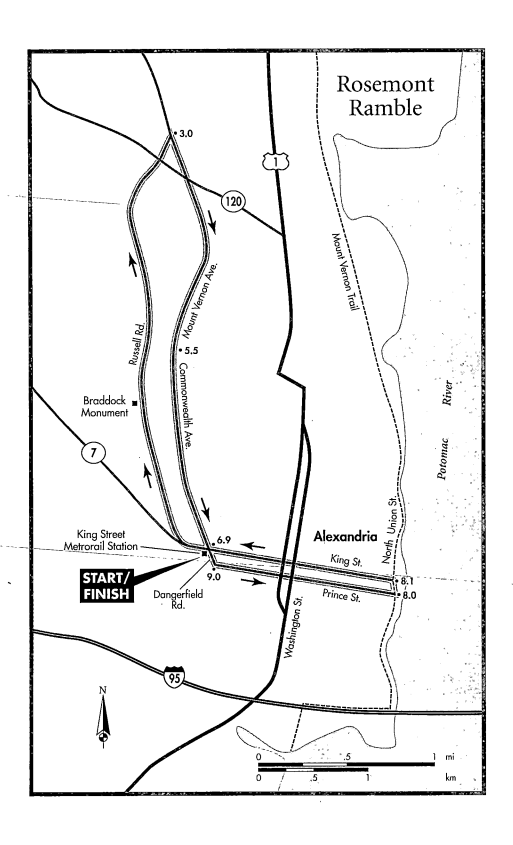

Rosemont Ramble

• 3.0

1

120

Mount Vernon Ave.

Russell Rd.

Mount Vernon Trail

• 5.5

Commonwealth Ave.

Braddock Monument

7

Potomac River

King Street Metrorail Station

North Union St.

Alexandria

• 6.9

King St.

START/ FINISH

9.0

Dangerfield Rd.

Prince St.

• 8.1
• 8.0

Washington St.

N

95

| 0 | | .5 | | 1 | mi |
| 0 | | .5 | | 1 | km |

0.0 From King Street Metro, go under tracks on King Street and bear right on Russell Road.

3.0 Follow Russell for about 30 blocks until it ends at Y intersection and take hard right on Mount Vernon Avenue.

5.5 At Y intersection, bear right on Commonwealth Avenue and follow for 25 blocks.

6.9 Pass under railroad tracks and turn left at light onto Daingerfield Road.

7.0 First left onto Prince Street.

8.0 Straight on Prince Street about 1 mile to North Union. Left onto North Union.

8.1 After 1 block, left onto King Street.

9.1 Straight for 1 mile back to King Street Metro station.

LOCAL EVENTS/ATTRACTIONS

♦ Historic Alexandria has events and attractions occurring year-round. Contact the chamber of commerce with the time of your visit for a detailed list.
♦ Torpedo Factory Art Center, 105 North Union Street, Alexandria, VA 22314; (703) 838–4565.

ACCOMMODATIONS

♦ Alexandria Hotel Association Accommodation, (800) 296–1000. This organization will check availability and rates, and make reservations at hotels.

BIKE SHOPS

♦ Big Wheel Bikes, 2 Prince Street, Alexandria, VA 22314; (703) 739–2300.

MAPS

♦ *Arlington, Virginia, Bikeway Map and Guide.* Published by the Arlington County Department of Public Works. Free. Contact Public Works Planning Division, No. 1 Court House Plaza, 2100 North Clarendon Boulevard, Arlington, VA 22201; (703) 228–3681.
♦ *Virginia Atlas and Gazetteer.* Published by DeLorme Mapping Company. Includes topographic maps, hike/bike trails, canoeing areas. $12.95. Available at bookstores.
♦ *ADC's Washington Area Bike Map.* Compiled by Metropolitan Washington Council of Governments. $10.95. Available at bookstores and newsstands.
♦ *D.C. Bikeways.* Series of maps published by the city. $3.00. Write to District of Columbia Office of Documents, 441 Fourth Street N.W., Suite 520, Washington, D.C. 20001; (202) 727–5090.

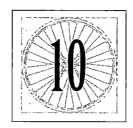

Reservoir—Great Falls Cruise

T his cruise alongside the snaking Potomac passes beautiful old homes on its way out to kayak country. The trail safely follows a wide shoulder that will take you in and out of the friendly shade of the tall trees that line the route. Throughout the length of the ride, you can find quaint places to stop and sip lemonade or look upon the Glen Echo amusement park.

This jaunt should be dedicated to Quartermaster General Montgomery C. Meigs, a Civil War hero and engineer who designed the 10-mile-long aqueduct system that still provides Washington with fresh water. In the process he created a refreshing route for modern-day cyclists. The Meigs legacy is announced by a series of whimsical structures that now line this popular cycling route to Great Falls National Park in Maryland.

Start at the confluence of Reservoir Road and MacArthur Boulevard, near a pumping structure that Meigs disguised as a classical temple. The reservoir's grounds are populated by black vultures, ducks, and even red foxes. You are in the heart of the city's Palisades enclave, dense with trees and rambling old wood-frame houses. Head west on MacArthur Boulevard, the neighborhood's main street, past such landmarks as a one-room schoolhouse and the Art Deco MacArthur Theater, now converted to a drugstore. The road is winding and busy, but the shoulder is wide and traffic moves slowly.

At the city line, marked by another reservoir, the boulevard narrows to a two-lane road. Switch to the bike path at left, parallel to oncoming traffic. Climb a short but steep hill to reach the Brookmont neighborhood. At the top of the hill, look to your right and you'll see the Capital Crescent Trail. You'll be riding over the Dalecarlia tunnel.

Next, the path traces a precipice high above the river. This was the old trolley route (described by John Dos Passos in his *U.S.A.* trilogy) from downtown to the country. Ruins of the old trestle remain among the sycamore trees and thorny undergrowth. For nearly seventy years the transit line's terminus was Glen Echo amusement park. After the park closed in 1968, the National Park Service acquired the land to create a cultural center. The 1921 Dentzel carousel has been restored, calliope intact, and is open spring through fall. Also preserved are the bumper-car shed and the Spanish Ballroom, still used for swing dances and concerts. This may be the world's only Art Deco ghost town—well worth a look. Reach Glen Echo by turning left onto Oxford Road, just past a small traffic circle.

Before leaving the streamlined spires of Glen Echo, visit the neighboring Clara Barton National Historic Site, a turreted Victorian house where the saintly founder of the American Red Cross spent her last fifteen years. It's open every day except national holidays.

Continuing west alongside MacArthur Boulevard, the trail meanders through the old town of Glen Echo. The historic Glen Echo Town Hall and Post Office are on your left, located on Harvard Avenue. Yes, there is also a Cornell Avenue, as well as Yale, Princeton, and Bryn Mawr. Take a short loop around the town and you'll encounter Oxford Road and Wellesley and Vassar Circles, too. Return to the bike path on MacArthur Boulevard, turn left, and continue through the town of Cabin John.

Slow down to cross a bridge wide enough for only one lane of cars and one lane of bicycles. This is Meigs's great 220-foot-long aqueduct, constructed to

Great Falls

convey 10,000 gallons of water hourly over the valley of Cabin John Creek. It still does the job—and carries rush-hour traffic in style as well.

A bit up the road on the right, hearty (and organic) human food is available at the Bethesda Co-op. The next landmark, on the left, is the U.S. Navy's Carderock Division of Naval Surface Warfare Center, which resembles a mile-long Quonset hut. The shed contains a tank for testing scale models of ships. Continue parallel to MacArthur Boulevard and its clusters of Victorian houses. These hills were once alive with gold mines, opened during the Civil War and abandoned since 1935.

By now cars will be whizzing by with splinter-shaped boats mounted on their roofs. These are kayakers heading for the mouth of Mather Gorge, whose rapids test the most competitive spirits. They put in near the C & O Canal right across from Old Angler's Inn, a tavern and restaurant since 1860. It's a pricey spot to take a break, but you may need the energy for the hill leading to the entrance to Great Falls Park. It's a long climb, so gear down and pedal easy to enjoy the smoothly paved road through deep woods.

Stay left at the top and zoom down the other side of the same hill to arrive at the Great Falls Tavern Visitor's Center. Be sure to stop at the guard house—there's an entrance fee of $2.00 for cyclists and $4.00 for cars. The tavern was built in 1890 to serve workers on the C & O Canal. Today it's a museum. Just across the canal, footpaths and platforms present views of this ferocious section of river, where in 0.25 mile rapids drop 76 feet through a gorge. Ask a local to point out the bald eagle nest on a river island.

Decision time: Either climb the steep hill back out of the park to double back to D.C. on the MacArthur Boulevard Trail, or return on the C & O Canal towpath, described in Ride 14.

Note: In 1996 a major flood breached the canal and ravaged its towpath. Temporary repairs were made, and the towpath is usually open. More permanent repairs continue, however, and you may encounter detours. Call the Great Falls Tavern Visitor's Center at (301) 299–3613 for up-to-date information.

LOCAL INFORMATION

♦ D.C. Chamber of Commerce, 1213 K Street N.W., Washington, D.C. 20005; (202) 347–7201.
♦ Conference and Visitors Bureau of Montgomery County, MD, Inc., 11820 Parklawn Drive, Suite 380, Rockville, MD 20852; (301) 428–9702 or (800) 925–0880.
♦ Montgomery County Recreation Department, 12210 Bushey Drive, Silver Spring, MD 20902; (240) 777–6804 (general information—recording).

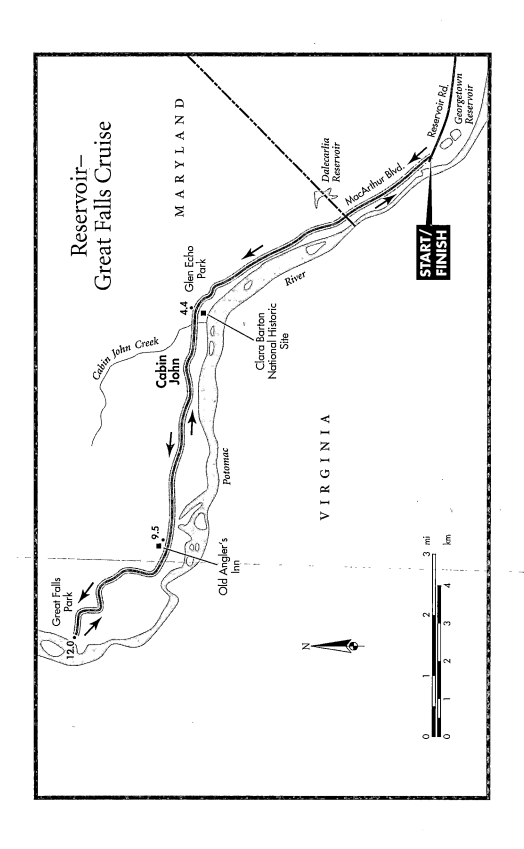

Reservoir–
Great Falls Cruise

MARYLAND

Dalecarlia
Reservoir

Reservoir Rd.

Georgetown
Reservoir

MacArthur Blvd.

START/
FINISH

Glen Echo
Park

4.4

Clara Barton
National Historic
Site

Cabin John Creek

Cabin
John

Potomac

River

Old Angler's
Inn

9.5

VIRGINIA

Great Falls
Park

12.0

N

3 mi
km

0.0 From MacArthur Boulevard and Reservoir Road, head west on shoulder of MacArthur. After passing Dalecarlia Reservoir, road narrows to two lanes. Cross MacArthur to off-road bike path that begins on left.

4.4 Follow bike path to parking area for Glen Echo Park and Clara Barton National Historic Site, about 4 miles from ride start.

9.5 Off-road path ends in another 5 miles. Follow on-road route as MacArthur Boulevard curves right past Old Angler's Inn for long, winding climb through the woods.

12.0 At crest of hill, turn left into Great Falls Park as Falls Road turns right. Swift descent on road leads to visitor center.

24.0 Retrace your steps to Washington. Or return via the C & O Canal towpath, a route that requires carrying your bike up and down several staircases on a walkway over the canal to avoid a rocky section near Great Falls. In 12 miles, at Fletcher's Boat House, cross the bridge over the canal. Cross Canal Road to Reservoir Road. Ride up a steep hill to the intersection of Reservoir and MacArthur (see Ride 14).

LOCAL EVENTS/ATTRACTIONS

◆ Clara Barton National Historic Site, 5801 Oxford Road, Glen Echo, MD 20812; (301) 492–6245; www.nps.gov/clba.
◆ Glen Echo Park, 7300 MacArthur Boulevard, Glen Echo, MD 20812; (301) 492–6229; www.nps.gov/glee.

ACCOMMODATIONS

◆ Old Angler's Inn, 10801 MacArthur Boulevard, Potomac, MD 20854; (301) 299–9097.
◆ Bed & Breakfast Accommodations, P.O. Box 12011, Washington, D.C. 20005; (202) 328–3510; www.bnbaccom.com.
◆ Washington D.C. Accommodations, 2201 Wisconsin Avenue, Suite C110, Washington, D.C. 20007; (202) 289–2220 or (800) 554–2220; www.wdcahotels. com.

BIKE SHOPS

◆ Revolution Cycles, at the foot of Key Bridge, 3411 M Street N.W., Washington, D.C.; (202) 965–3601.
◆ The Bicycle Pro Shop, 3403 M Street N.W., Washington, D.C. 20007; (202) 337–0311.

◆ Big Wheel Bikes, 1034 Thirty-third Street N.W., Washington, D.C.; (202) 337–0254.

MAPS

◆ *ADC's Washington Area Bike Map.* Compiled by Metropolitan Washington Council of Governments. $10.95. Available at bookstores and newsstands.
◆ *D.C. Bikeways.* Series of maps published by the city. $3.00. Write to District of Columbia Office of Documents, 441 Fourth Street N.W., Suite 520, Washington, D.C. 20001; (202) 727–5090.
◆ *Maryland Bicycle Touring Map.* Free. Available from Office of Tourism Development, 45 Calvert Street, Annapolis, MD 21401.
◆ *Trails in Montgomery County Parks.* Contact Maryland–National Capital Park and Planning Commission (MNCPPC), 8787 Georgia Avenue N.W., Silver Spring, MD 20910; (301) 495–2503.

Upper Rock Creek Park Ramble

T he upper reaches of Rock Creek park are a natural paradise to the city cyclists. This ride is especially peaceful and traffic-free during the weekends when the park police close Beach Drive to traffic. If you don't mind sharing the trail with folks having the same idea as you, the hilly ride will almost make you feel like you're in the country.

This is Rock Creek's more rustic side. The park's 1,800 acres are 85 percent wooded and contain fifteen wildflower meadows comprised of 400 plant species, including goldenrod, purpletop grass, thistle, and aster. A British ambassador once asked rhetorically, "What city in the world is there where a man can, within a quarter of an hour and on his own feet, get in a beautiful rocky glen such as you would find in the woods of Maine or Scotland?" Here Theodore Roosevelt would go off on rugged jaunts, and John Quincy Adams described visiting "this romantic glen, listening to the singing of a thousand birds."

Among the glades and dells of Rock Creek are great stands of tulip trees, oak, and dogwood, with an understory of alder bush, azalea, and witch hazel. The park roads have been designed to follow the undulations of these hills. Dramatic, sweeping curves provide excellent views of the gorge. Bridle paths cross the roadbeds at many intervals. Traffic is light except on Beach Drive, a busy commuter road on weekdays that is closed to motor traffic on weekends and holidays (see Ride 4). An off-road trail runs parallel to the portion of Beach Drive included in this ride.

Start next to the rumbling falls at historic Pierce Mill. Proceed north through the parking area with Rock Creek on your right. In 0.25 mile turn left onto two-lane Broad Branch Road and take an immediate right onto Ridge Road. Climb a steep hill for 0.5 mile. Note the rustic stone wall on the S curve.

Pass a rambling meadow retained by a split-log fence.

Bear left at a sign for the nature center to traverse a broad meadow with playing fields and picnic tables. Come to an intersection with a traffic light. Cross four-lane Military Road (an important Civil War supply line) to reach Oregon Avenue. (Or take the marked off-road path that runs parallel.) This two-lane road divides a residential neighborhood from the dense woods of Rock Creek Park's western border. The rambling houses on the left are among the city's most exclusive, combining bucolic pleasures with a short commute to downtown D.C. On the right are the ruins of Fort DeRussy at the park's highest point. A hike into the woods will reveal the remains of earthworks, moats, and trenches from this Civil War site.

At Bingham Drive turn right and hang on for a steep descent to the Rock Creek basin. You can choose between the roadbed (smooth surface, no shoulders, moderate traffic) and the path at left (separate from traffic, fair surface). At Beach Drive, to avoid heavy traffic, turn right onto a much smoother off-road trail. Continue along the valley floor for about 1 mile to Joyce Road, a four-way stop. Turn right and immediately left onto Ross Drive. Prepare for several steep climbs and descents through wooded highlands. Near the nature center Ross Drive melts into Ridge Road. Like all good rides, this one ends with a sharp descent. Slow down for the S curve around a picnic meadow, and return to Pierce Mill.

Option: To connect to Rock Creek Regional Park in Maryland and avoid weekday traffic on Beach Drive, keep straight on Oregon rather than turning right onto Bingham Drive. Follow Oregon until it ends at Western Avenue, and turn left. Shortly thereafter turn right onto Greenvale Street. In a few blocks turn left onto Beach Drive. Cross the bridge at Candy Cane City, a playground next to the Meadowbrook Riding Stables, to reach the Maryland bikeway through Rock Creek Regional Park, described in Ride 4. It runs about 16 miles to Lake Needwood.

LOCAL INFORMATION

♦ D.C. Chamber of Commerce, 1213 K Street N.W., Washington, D.C. 20005; (202) 347–7201.
♦ Conference and Visitors Bureau of Montgomery County, MD, Inc., 11820 Parklawn Drive, Suite 380, Rockville, MD 20852; (301) 428–9702 or (800) 925–0880.
♦ Montgomery County Recreation Department, 12210 Bushey Drive, Silver Spring, MD 20902; (240) 777–6804 (general information—recording).

LOCAL EVENTS/ATTRACTIONS

♦ Rock Creek Park, Washington, D.C., www.nps.gov. Luckily for Washingtonians, in 1890 Congress prevented this 1,800-acre green valley that cuts a swathe from Georgetown north through the city to the Maryland state line from becoming the unofficial city dump. Today this tranquil urban valley is a haven for bikers, joggers, and picnickers. It is a place where people can enjoy themselves, sitting quietly under the shade trees along the banks of the creek, cooking over a barbecue grill or enjoying the sight and fragrance of the daffodils and other flowers that bloom here each spring.
♦ Rock Creek Park Nature Center & Planetarium, 5200 Glover Road N.W., Washington, D.C.; (202) 426–6829. A spot where you can see live and mounted wildlife displays, environmental exhibits, and planetarium shows, as well as participate in guided nature walks. For horseback-riding lessons, visit the Horse Centre off Military Road at 5100 Glover Road N.W. Call (202) 362–0117.

ACCOMMODATIONS

♦ Bed & Breakfast Accommodations, P.O. Box 12011, Washington, D.C. 20005; (202) 328–3510; www.bnbaccom.com.
♦ Washington D.C. Accommodations, 2201 Wisconsin Avenue, Suite C110, Washington, D.C. 20007; (202) 289–2220 or (800) 554–2220; www.wdcahotels.com.
♦ Bethesda Marriott Hotel, 5151 Pooks Hill Road, Bethesda, MD 20814; (301) 897–9400 or (800) 228–9290; fax (301) 897–4156.
♦ Holiday Inn Select Bethesda, 8120 Wisconsin Avenue, Bethesda, MD 20814; (301) 652–2000 or (800) HOLIDAY; fax (301) 652–4525.

BIKE SHOPS

♦ Revolution Cycles, at the foot of Key Bridge, 3411 M Street N.W., Washington, D.C. 20007; (202) 965–3601.
♦ The Bicycle Pro Shop, 3403 M Street N.W., Washington, D.C. 20007; (202) 337–0311.

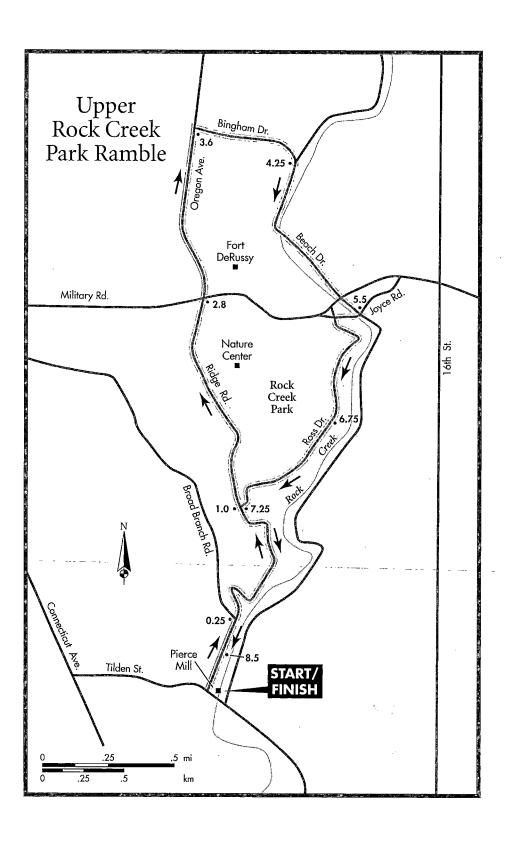

Upper
Rock Creek
Park Ramble

Bingham Dr.
• 3.6
4.25 •

Oregon Ave.

Fort
DeRussy
■

Beach Dr.

Military Rd.
• 2.8
5.5 •
Joyce Rd.

Nature
Center
■

Ridge Rd.

Rock
Creek
Park

Ross Dr.
• 6.75

Rock Creek

16th St.

Broad Branch Rd.

1.0 • • 7.25

N

Connecticut Ave.

0.25 •

Tilden St.
Pierce
Mill
• • 8.5

START/
FINISH

0   .25   .5 mi
0   .25   .5   km

0.0 Head north from Pierce Mill parking area.
0.25 Go left onto Broad Branch Road and immediately right onto Ridge Road.
1.0 Bear left at sign for nature center as Ross Drive turns right.
2.8 At Military Road traffic light, go straight. Ridge Road becomes Oregon Avenue.
3.6 Right onto Bingham Drive.
4.25 Right onto off-road trail parallel to Beach Drive. On weekends Beach Drive is closed to vehicular traffic.
5.5 At four-way stop, right onto Joyce Road.
6.75 First left onto Ross Drive.
7.0 Ross Drive ends at Ridge Road near nature center. Turn left.
7.25 Left at bottom of long hill.
8.5 Right into Pierce Mill parking area.

♦ Big Wheel Bikes, 1034 Thirty-third Street N.W., Washington, D.C. 20007; (202) 337–0254.
♦ Big Wheel Bikes, 6917 Arlington Road, Bethesda, MD 20814; (301) 652–0192.

MAPS

♦ *ADC's Washington Area Bike Map.* Compiled by Metropolitan Washington Council of Governments. $10.95. Available at bookstores and newsstands.
♦ *D.C. Bikeways.* Series of maps published by the city. $3.00. Write to District of Columbia Office of Documents, 441 Fourth Street N.W., Suite 520, Washington, D.C. 20001; (202) 727–5090.
♦ *Maryland Bicycle Touring Map.* Free. Available from Office of Tourism Development, 45 Calvert Street, Annapolis, MD 21401.
♦ *Trails in Montgomery County Parks.* Contact Maryland–National Capital Park and Planning Commission (MNCPPC), 8787 Georgia Avenue N.W., Silver Spring, MD 20910; (301) 495–2503; www.mncppc.org.

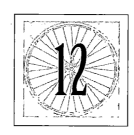

Sligo–Rock Creek Weekend Ramble

T hink quick escape. If you live in D.C., Bethesda, Silver Spring, or Takoma Park, you can do this ride without loading the roof rack or jumping on the subway. This is my after-gardening-but-before-dinner ride. Combining aspects of Rides 4 and 21, it melds routes through two stream-valley parks with looks at two historic areas not covered elsewhere here. It's a weekend-only ride because it includes sections of Beach Drive that are closed to cars Saturday and Sunday but packed with commuters on weekdays.

Start at the intersection of Beach and Sherrill Drives in the D.C. portion of Rock Creek Park, about 2 miles north of the National Zoo. Head north past picnic areas, rock outcroppings, and stands of mountain laurel (the pink and white blooms come out in late May). Horse trails parallel this route, along with hiking trails maintained by the Potomac Appalachian Trail Club. Lock up your bike sometime and try one—it's easy to lose the city within the park's 1,800 acres.

Most but not all of Beach Drive is closed on weekends; a few sections remain open so that groups can reach picnic areas by car. Beware of the occasional auto. After leaving the city through a bikes-only gate, look for a playground called Candy Cane City. A marked sign on the right leads off Beach Drive and over a small bridge. Turn left into a parking lot and pass the playground and ball fields until you reach a T next to a horse pasture; this is the Meadowbrook Stable. Turn left onto Meadowbrook Lane until you come to East-West Highway, a major arterial. Cross at the signal to pick up a bike path that heads north past playing fields and wetlands. Proceed to the Walter Reed Annex as described in Ride 4 (Rock Creek Park: To Maryland and Back). This

time you'll pass through the architectural theme park. At the top of
the winding bike path, turn left onto
Linden Lane and bear right at the
next fork (signed bike route).

Coast down a hill (past Ye Forest
Inne, a failed resort in the 1890s and
now part of Walter Reed Annex) to
cross the Beltway on an overpass
and cruise through the historic
community of Forest Glen.
Founded by the notable Carroll
family in the 1700s among a 4,200-
acre tract of wilderness, Forest Glen
retains a country feel, with winding
roads and old frame houses with
broad porches. On the left St. John's
Cemetery doubles as a village green.
The road is tight, but the drivers
courteous. At the top of the hill are
railroad tracks and the former B &
O railroad station.

After passing the new Forest
Glen Metrorail station, cross busy
Georgia Avenue at the signal and
descend past Holy Cross Hospital
on the right. Bear right at the bottom of the hill to pick up the Sligo Creek
Hiker-Biker Trail.

Environmentally speaking, Sligo Creek has long been a poor sister to the
wider, better-preserved Rock Creek Valley, but that may be changing. (It's hard
to believe that the sometimes foul-smelling Sligo supplied water mains until
1930.) The local sewer commission plans to remove leaky pipes (think the
worst) from the creekbed to a new right-of-way above the banks. Many new
trees, including lovely paperbark birches, have been planted in the park, and
wildflower meadows have supplanted boring expanses of lawn. Parts of the
creek banks are being restored with native vegetation, and the number of fish
species living in Sligo Creek is expected to jump from one to a dozen or so.
Recently the hiker-biker trail was extended 3.3 miles east, where it meets the
trailhead of Northwest Branch (see Ride 21).

Ride on the parkway if traffic isn't too bad, or on the winding bike path if
it is. There are places where the retrofitted bike path crosses very narrow
bridges and takes sharp turns. Let your sense of caution be your guide. At
Maple Avenue turn right to pass by Takoma Park's high-rise apartment district.

This section ends at the Sam Abbott Municipal Center, named for the late rabble-rousing mayor, a socialist who fought proposed highways that would have destroyed Takoma Park. He once said, "It doesn't bother me at all that I don't have suburban decorum." Next door is a friendly city library—the only one in Maryland outside of Baltimore.

Go straight to enter the Takoma Park Historic District. Founded in 1976 in the wake of highway and other development battles, the historic district embraces parts of D.C. and two Maryland counties. The city was carved out of farms and wilderness in 1883 by developer Benjamin Franklin Gilbert; in 1904 it took off in a spurt when the Seventh-Day Adventist Church moved from Battle Creek, Michigan, to make Takoma its headquarters. (SDA has since moved to sober corporate headquarters in Silver Spring, leaving in its righteous wake an almost publess, dry Takoma.)

A ride up Maple Avenue reveals large, four-square homes mixed in with gingerbread Victorians dating back to the 1890s. Many have been restored. An original city boundary marker (circa 1791) sits behind an iron fence near Maple and Carroll Avenues. Turn left down Tulip Avenue to the main drag, Carroll Avenue. Here is the heart of Washington's "folk ghetto," the House of Musical Traditions, where you can buy a hammer dulcimer or take lessons in African drumming, along with other craft shops, bookstores, and restaurants. A Sunday farmers' market (in season) makes a cycling destination—bring panniers.

Follow Carroll Avenue (Route 195) as it turns right toward the Takoma Metro station. Take Butternut Street N.W. in D.C. At Georgia Avenue go straight across the street and turn right onto the sidewalk to ride around the Walter Reed Army Medical Center, founded in 1898. This formal campus mixes Georgian architecture with modern and features one major public attraction: the National Museum of Health and Medicine, repository of the bullet that killed Lincoln, along with other medical curios and scientific exhibits. Until the late 1960s this was one of the most popular museums on the Mall; to make room for the Hirshhorn Museum, the redbrick building was razed and the collection exiled to Walter Reed.

Turn left onto Fern Street, staying on the sidewalk until you reach the Alaska Avenue Gate. Take a left onto Alaska Avenue and another left onto Sixteenth (traffic—use the sidewalk) to Sherrill Drive. Turn right and head downhill to return to the ride's starting point.

LOCAL INFORMATION

♦ D.C. Chamber of Commerce, 1213 K Street N.W., Washington, D.C. 20005; (202) 347–7201.

♦ Conference and Visitors Bureau of Montgomery County, MD, Inc., 11820 Parklawn Drive, Suite 380, Rockville, MD 20852; (301) 428–9702 or (800) 925–0880.

B&O Railroad Station

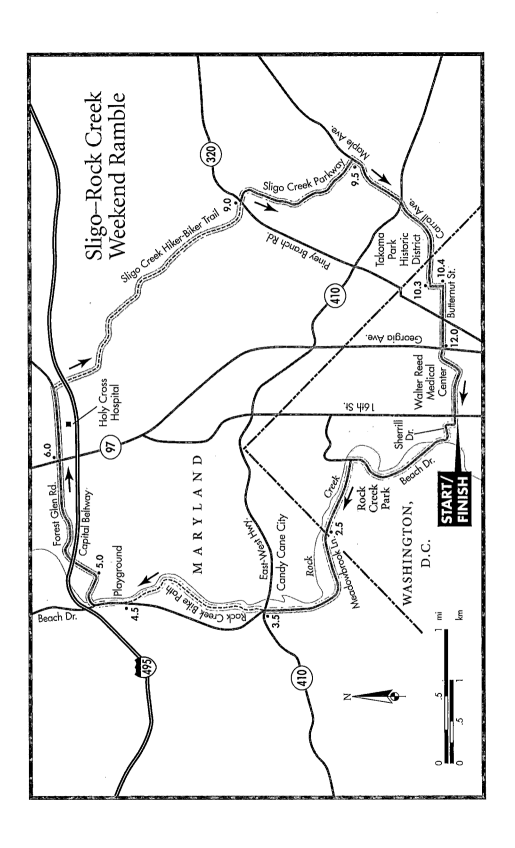

Sligo–Rock Creek
Weekend Ramble

Sligo Creek Hiker-Biker Trail

320

9.0

Sligo Creek Parkway

9.5

Maple Ave.

Piney Branch Rd.

410

Carroll Ave.

Takoma
Park
Historic
District

10.3

10.4

Butternut St.

Georgia Ave.

12.0

Walter Reed
Medical
Center

16th St.

Sherrill
Dr.

Holy Cross
Hospital

6.0

97

Forest Glen Rd.

Capital Beltway

5.0

Playground

4.5

Beach Dr.

495

Rock Creek Bike Path

MARYLAND

East-West Hwy.

Candy Cane City

3.5

Rock

Creek

Rock
Creek
Park

Beach Dr.

Meadowbrook Ln.

2.5

WASHINGTON,
D.C.

START/
FINISH

410

N

1 mi

km

0

0

.5

1

.5

1

0.0 From Sherrill Drive, right onto Beach Drive to head north.

2.5 From Beach Drive, turn right to enter Candy Cane City playground. Bear left and follow bike-route signs out of parking lot.

2.6 Left at T onto Meadowbrook Lane.

3.5 Cross East-West Highway (Route 410) to pick up Rock Creek bike path north.

4.5 Turn right past small playground to take path to Walter Reed Annex.

5.0 Left onto Linden Lane. Follow bike route signs across Beltway and railroad tracks. At top of hill, where sign reads BIKE ROUTE ENDS (ignore it), go straight to pick up Forest Glen Road through historic Forest Glen.

6.0 Cross Georgia Avenue at signal to stay on Forest Glen Road for another 6 blocks.

7.0 After passing Holy Cross Hospital on right, turn right onto Sligo Creek Hiker-Biker Trail.

9.0 After crossing Piney Branch at signal, go straight onto Sligo Creek Parkway (caution—narrow road with traffic) or stay on winding bike path.

9.5 At T, right onto Maple Avenue.

10.1 At four-way stop, left onto Tulip Avenue.

10.3 In 3 blocks at T, right onto Carroll Avenue. At Takoma clock tower, turn right to stay on Carroll Avenue. Stay on Carroll through underpass beneath Metrorail tracks. At signal immediately after underpass, left onto Fourth Street N.W.

10.4 In 1 block, right onto Butternut Street N.W.

12.0 At Georgia Avenue, cross at signal and turn right onto sidewalk around Walter Reed Medical Center.

12.2 Staying on sidewalk, turn left onto Fern Street to Alaska Avenue Gate.

12.4 Left onto Alaska Avenue N.W.

12.6 Left onto Sixteenth Street (traffic).

13.0 First right onto Sherrill Drive. Return to start.

♦ Montgomery County Recreation Department, 12210 Bushey Drive, Silver Spring, MD 20902; (240) 777–6804 (general information—recording).

LOCAL EVENTS/ATTRACTIONS

♦ Rock Creek Park, Washington, D.C.; www.nps.gov. Luckily for Washingtonians, in 1890 Congress prevented this 1,800-acre green valley that cuts a swathe from Georgetown north through the city to the Maryland state line from becoming the unofficial city dump. Today this tranquil urban valley is a haven for bikers, joggers, and picnickers. It is a place where people can enjoy themselves, sitting quietly under the shade trees along the banks of the creek, cooking over a barbecue grill, or enjoying the sight and fragrance of the daffodils and other flowers that bloom here each spring.

♦ Rock Creek Park Nature Center & Planetarium, 5200 Glover Road N.W., Washington, D.C.; (202) 426–6829. A spot where you can see live and mounted wildlife displays, environmental exhibits, and planetarium shows, as well as participate in guided nature walks. For horseback-riding lessons, visit the Horse Centre off Military Road at 5100 Glover Road N.W. Call (202) 362–0117.

ACCOMMODATIONS

♦ Bed & Breakfast Accommodations, P.O. Box 12011, Washington, D.C. 20005; (202) 328–3510; www.bnbaccom.com.

♦ Washington D.C. Accommodations, 2201 Wisconsin Avenue, Suite C110, Washington, D.C. 20007; (202) 289–2220 or (800) 554–2220; www.wdcahotels.com.

♦ Bethesda Marriott Hotel, 5151 Pooks Hill Road, Bethesda, MD 20814; (301) 897–9400 or (800) 228–9290; fax (301) 897–4156.

♦ Holiday Inn Select Bethesda, 8120 Wisconsin Avenue, Bethesda, MD 20814; (301) 652–2000 or (800) HOLIDAY; fax (301) 652–4525.

BIKE SHOPS

♦ Revolution Cycles, at the foot of Key Bridge, 3411 M Street N.W., Washington, D.C. 20007; (202) 965–3601.

♦ The Bicycle Pro Shop, 3403 M Street N.W., Washington, D.C. 20007; (202) 337–0311.

♦ Big Wheel Bikes, 1034 Thirty-third Street N.W., Washington, D.C.; (202) 337–0254.

♦ Big Wheel Bikes, 6917 Arlington Road, Bethesda, MD 20814; (301) 652–0192.

MAPS

♦ *ADC's Washington Area Bike Map*. Compiled by Metropolitan Washington Council of Governments. $10.95. Available at bookstores and newsstands.

♦ *D.C. Bikeways*. Series of maps published by the city. $3.00. Write to District of Columbia Office of Documents, 441 Fourth Street N.W., Suite 520, Washington, D.C. 20001; (202) 727–5090.

♦ *Maryland Bicycle Touring Map*. Free. Available from Office of Tourism Development, 45 Calvert Street, Annapolis, MD 21401.

♦ *Trails in Montgomery County Parks*. Contact Maryland–National Capital Park and Planning Commission (MNCPPC), 8787 Georgia Avenue N.W., Silver Spring, MD 20910; (301) 495–2503.

National Arboretum
Loop-de-Loop Ramble

T his ramble never ceases to amaze me—it's different all year round. The ride is all within a small area and crosses back upon itself mazelike. Things bloom at every turn spring and summer long. There are few cars, if any, and minimal crowds to contend with. The road surface is well kept and smooth. One of the beauties of the arbore-tum is its rolling land, which lends itself well to bicycle riding. You can cruise downhill while gazing at the blur of color passing by on each side of you.

Washington has long been known as the City of Trees. Most neighborhoods are lined by oaks, sycamores, or even ginkgo trees, and the April blooming of the Japanese cherry trees draws millions of tourists. But the most impressive year-round display can be found at the 444-acre National Arboretum in the midst of gritty Northeast Washington. Here the prevailing mood falls between virgin forest and formal garden. Many of the trees, shrubs, and herbs are so rare they attract visitors from throughout the world.

Founded in 1927 under the auspices of the U.S. Department of Agriculture, the arboretum blooms from March through October. In winter the colors become considerably more muted, but the collection of dwarf conifers, the frozen ponds, and the tall wheat-colored grasses make off-season visits worth-while. Summer visitors are rewarded by the sight of vast lily pads with their pink and white blooms. Ostensibly a research facility for botanists, the arbore-tum is one of the more graceful and serene parks in Washington.

This suggested tour loops around the grounds three times to cover most of

The National Arboretum

its 9 miles of lightly traveled roads. Many are unmarked, so you may find it difficult to follow this route exactly. All the roads are bikable, though. If you miss a turn, just follow the signs back to the gift shop. You can pick up a *Visitor's Guide*, which includes an excellent map.

The ride starts near the National Bonsai Collection. Housed in a Japanese-style pavilion, the bonsai trees are up to 350 years old but only a few feet high. Their disposition results from generations of careful "training" by Japanese horticulturists, who donated their life's work in honor of our bicentennial. These tiny ginkgoes, maples, spruces, and crab apples form an alluring landscape in miniature.

Starting just past the gift shop at the entrance, the ride begins with a steep climb up to a precipice with a view of the mausoleums of historic Mt. Olivet Cemetery across Bladensburg Road. In spring the 65,000 azaleas on this hillock burst out in pink, purple, orange, and scarlet blooms. There's also a stand of a type of dawn redwood that exists nowhere else outside China. Cruising downhill at high speed, pass flowering crab apples and a bird garden. The road continues to descend into a dark valley of ferns. Cross a streambed and bear right at a pond (often full of geese) to climb again for a view of the Anacostia River. This slow-moving tidal branch of the Potomac is here seen at its bucolic best.

Heading north, the cyclist encounters Japanese, Korean, and Chinese gardens complemented by pagodas, bridges, and other structures of the East. A cruise past neat rows of Japanese maples completes the first leg. Starting again from the parking area, repeat the first section of the ride until reaching Beech Spring Pond, where you turn left instead of bearing right. Near a second pond, by a fragrant area of lilacs and hibiscus, turn right to cross a broad meadow. Take the next two left turns to traverse what looks like pristine farmland on the way back to the start.

The final leg affords a look at a hillside planted with 1,500 dwarf conifers such as yew, cedar, and pine. Like the bonsai, the dwarf conifers have been sculpted into shapely miniatures. Unlike the potted Japanese trees, they are

THE BASICS

Start: National Arboretum

Distance: 9-mile loop

Approximate pedaling time: 1 hour

Terrain and surface: Rolling hills; smooth roads

Things to see: Bonsai collection, azalea garden, U.S. Capitol columns, Anacostia River, ponds and streams

Traffic and hazards: None

Facilities: Rest rooms at gift shop and Japanese Gardens

Getting there: From Capitol Hill, take Maryland Avenue to M Street entrance. From downtown, take New York Avenue to service road on right after Bladensburg Road. From Maryland, take Route 50 west to New York Avenue and follow signs to service road. Park at information center and gift shop.

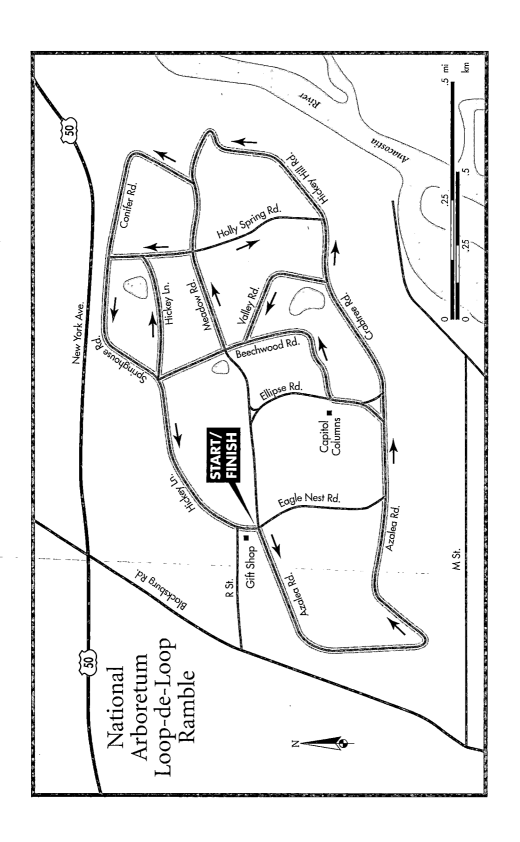

National
Arboretum
Loop-de-Loop
Ramble

START/
FINISH

Capitol
Columns

Gift Shop

New York Ave.

Springhouse Rd.

Conifer Rd.

Hickey Ln.

Meadow Rd.

Holly Spring Rd.

Valley Rd.

Hickey Hill Rd.

Crabtree Rd.

Beechwood Rd.

Ellipse Rd.

Eagle Nest Rd.

Azalea Rd.

Azalea Rd.

Hickey Ln.

Blacksburg Rd.

R St.

M St.

Anacostia

River

.5 mi
km

.5

.25

.5

.25

0
0

N

Note: Use blocks and features instead of miles for navigation.
- By bike, head west on Azalea Road past gift shop.
- At Rhododendron Valley Road, bear left to stay on Azalea Road.
- Azalea Road becomes Crabtree Road.
- At pond, bear right onto Hickey Hill Road.
- At Y intersection, bear right onto Conifer Road.
- At Y intersection, bear left and then right onto Hickey Lane. Return to start.
- Head west on Azalea Road.
- At pond, bear left onto Valley Road.
- Right onto Meadow Road.
- Bear left at Y intersection.
- Left onto Conifer Road and return to start.
- West on Azalea Road.
- Left onto Ellipse Road to see U.S. Capitol columns.
- Right onto Beechwood Road.
- Right onto Meadow Road.
- Left onto Holly Spring Road.
- Left onto Conifer Road and return to start.

planted in the ground, giving the impression of a troll forest. Another quirky feature on the grounds is the collection of the original Corinthian columns from the east portico of the U.S. Capitol. The columns were dismantled in the 1950s when the east front was remodeled. They were re-erected here in 1990 in their original configuration—freestanding columns eerily girding nothing. The latest addition to the arboretum is a collection of bonsai trained in North America. Two projects are on the boards: a National Bird Garden and a National Grove of State Trees.

Except in spring, when the azaleas burst, the arboretum is never as crowded as other Washington attractions. The roads all run one-way. Since most people walk the grounds, you won't encounter many automobiles. The only drawback is that the arboretum is not easily reached by bike paths, on-road routes, or Metrorail.

LOCAL INFORMATION

- D.C. Chamber of Commerce, 1213 K Street N.W., Washington, D.C. 20005; (202) 347–7201.

LOCAL EVENTS/ATTRACTIONS

◆ United States National Arboretum, Twenty-fourth and R Street N.E., Washington, D.C.; (202) 245–2726. Open from 8:00 A.M. to 5:00 P.M. daily. A living museum, the arboretum is a forested wonderland promoting improved floral and landscape plants through research and education. It contains the National Bonsai Collection, a gift from the Nippon Bonsai Collection, which can be viewed from 10:00 A.M. to 3:30 P.M., and the Japanese Garden, a gift to commemorate America's bicentennial. Dont miss the Herbarium (500,000 dried plants all grown in the National Herb Garden), the Gtelli Dwarf Conifer Collection, or the Carl Buchheister National Bird Garden. Walk along nature trails. Enjoy beautiful ponds and streams that wind through groupings of foreign and domestic trees. There is no admission fee.

ACCOMMODATIONS

◆ Bed & Breakfast Accommodations, P.O. Box 12011, Washington, D.C. 20005; (202) 328–3510; www.bnbaccom.com.
◆ Washington D.C. Accommodations, 2201 Wisconsin Avenue, Suite C110, Washington, D.C. 20007; (202) 289–2220 or (800) 554–2220; www.wdca hotels.com.

MAPS

◆ *ADC's Washington Area Bike Map.* Compiled by Metropolitan Washington Council of Governments. $10.95. Available at bookstores and newsstands.
◆ *D.C. Bikeways.* Series of maps published by the city. $3.00. Write to District of Columbia Office of Documents, 441 Fourth Street N.W., Suite 520, Washington, D.C. 20001; (202) 727–5090.

C & O Canal Ramble

GEORGETOWN TO GREAT FALLS

his dirt ramble is a great escape and readily accessible from pretty much everywhere in the area. Mostly flat, it's a very popular trail on weekends with families and Georgetown locals. Riding a couple of miles out of Georgetown, you'll leave behind the crowds with baby strollers and bird-watching books. It's quite flat, enabling even the newest of beginners to take advantage of this very enjoyable ride.

The Chesapeake & Ohio Canal was destined to be a financial flop even before the first spadeful of earth was turned in 1828. The reason: the rise of railroads. By 1850, when canal construction stretched 184 miles from Georgetown in Washington to Cumberland, Maryland, in the Appalachian Mountains, freight trains had siphoned away much of the canal's business.

In 1924 the obsolete canal closed for good. In the 1950s even the Washington Post advocated filling in the remains to create a new commuter road. In stepped U.S. Supreme Court Justice William O. Douglas, an avid birder and hiker who led a cavalcade of decision makers on a nature walk that changed many minds. In 1977 President Jimmy Carter dedicated the C & O Canal National Historic Park in honor of Douglas.

The route follows the unpaved towpath, designed for mules to pull oblong barges carrying coal down the canal. Though bumpy in places (skinny tires, beware), the path offers many rewards for cyclists, joggers, and birders. Today mules still pull replicas of the old canal barges for pleasure rides down the canal. Injecting a linear slice of nature right into the city, the canal is lined by a canopy of sycamore, red maple, sassafras, and willow trees, along with mushrooms, wild raspberries, and wildflowers such as blue phlox, Queen Anne's

Start: Thompson Boat Center

Distance: 15 miles, one way

Approximate pedaling time: 3 hours

Terrain and surface: Flat; packed dirt with some rocks

Things to see: Working locks of nineteenth-century canal, rapids and dams of Potomac River, lock keepers' houses and other historic structures

Traffic and hazards: No traffic; mostly loose gravel trails

Facilities: Rest room, snacks, bike and canoe rentals, fishing gear at Fletcher's Boat House and Swain's Lock; snacks and boat rides at Great Falls

Options: Extend ride to Seneca, Maryland; return via MacArthur Boulevard; join Ride 26; join Ride 25

Getting there: From north, Rock Creek Parkway to Thompson's parking lot; turn right. From Mall, Virginia Avenue west across Rock Creek Parkway to Thompson's parking lot. From Virginia, Theodore Roosevelt or Memorial Bridge to Rock Creek Parkway to Thompson's parking lot. By Metro, Blue or Orange Line to Foggy Bottom/GWU, about 1-mile walk via New Hampshire and Virginia Avenues.

lace, and mayapples. The bird density is three times that of the regional average. While pedaling my mountain bike at 15 miles per hour, I've spotted barred owls, pileated woodpeckers, red-tailed hawks, and bluebirds. Spouts that bypass the locks create little falls rumbling over boulders. Turnarounds for barges have degraded into freshwater swamps full of cattails and hawk roosts. The still, opaque waters of the canal itself are alive with carp and turtles.

Canal cruisers will begin their rides at the Harry T. Thompson Boat Center, the starting point for many rides described in this book. Turn left out of the parking lot and left again onto a brick path marked as the beginning of the C & O park. Passing through Georgetown, you'll encounter the first canal lock. This begins a ride to Great Falls headed ever-so-slightly uphill—a total of 190 feet in 15 miles. The entire route is restored with working locks and charming fieldstone lock keepers' houses. Brown mile markers along the way make it easy to find canal highlights and ruins. For example:

Mile 0: The towpath passes under the grand arches of Key Bridge. Francis Scott Key actually lived near here in a mansion dismantled in the 1940s. A footpath leads up to M Street and the many shops and historic houses of the old port of Georgetown.

Mile 0.1: Next to a vast green boathouse in Georgetown, find the remains of the Old Alexandria Aqueduct, which spanned the Potomac. This is also the starting point for the Capital Crescent Trail, which follows an old railroad right-of-way to downtown Bethesda. See Ride 5 for a complete loop incorporating this rail-to-trail stretch.

Mile 1.8: Look across the Potomac for a view of a wet-weather waterfall on the Virginia side.

C & O Towpath Bridge crossing

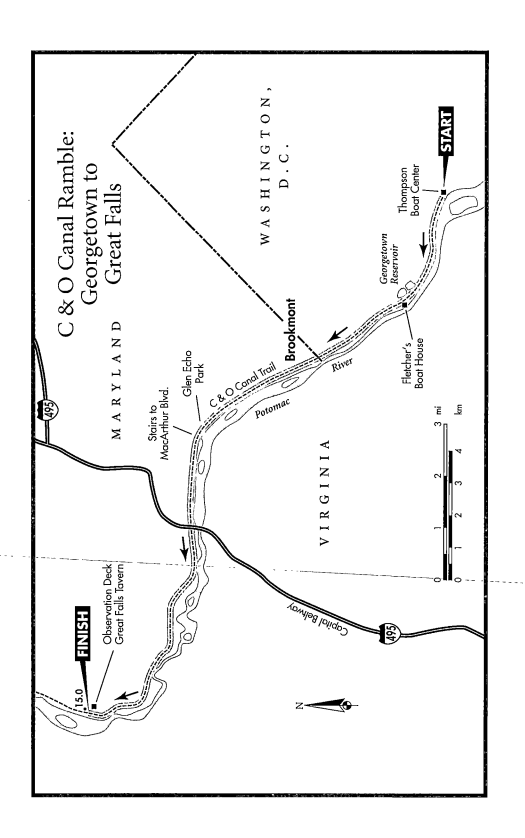

C & O Canal Ramble:
Georgetown to
Great Falls

START

Thompson
Boat Center

Georgetown
Reservoir

Fletcher's
Boat House

Brookmont

C & O Canal Trail

River

Potomac

Stairs to
MacArthur Blvd.

Glen Echo
Park

MARYLAND

WASHINGTON,
D.C.

VIRGINIA

Capital Beltway

495

495

FINISH

15.0

Observation Deck
Great Falls Tavern

N

0   1   2   3 mi

0   1   2   3   4 km

0.0 Exit Thompson Boat Center toward Rock Creek Parkway. Turn left immediately onto Rock Creek bike path.

0.1 After crossing concrete bridge, turn left onto brick trail. This is the trailhead for the towpath of C & O Canal.
– After crossing Twenty-eighth and Twenty-ninth Streets in Georgetown, trail becomes packed dirt.
– At Thirty-fourth Street, cross footbridge to other side of canal. Trail continues on Potomac River side.

15.0 Follow milestones to Great Falls. *Note:* Cyclists must dismount and walk near Great Falls for about 0.25 mile.

Options:

♦ You may return via the route described in Ride 10 by taking the park road up the hill out of Great Falls. At top of hill, turn right onto MacArthur Boulevard. Then right onto Chain Bridge Road to pick up C & O Canal for return to Thompson's.

♦ You may join Ride 26 by continuing on the towpath to White's Ferry, Maryland.

♦ You may join Ride 25 by continuing past Great Falls to Pennyfield Lock Road. Turn right onto Pennyfield, climb a hill, and turn left onto River Road.

Mile 2.4: Another boathouse with a country flavor, Fletcher's, rents mountain bikes, boats, and fishing gear.

Mile 2.7: Pass under the old B & O railroad bridge, which now carries the Capital Crescent Trail away from the river, across the canal.

Mile 4.7: The "feeder" draws water from the river to discharge into the canal at lock 5. Look closely at the curved red sandstone of the locks to find initials and symbols carved in by the stonecutters.

Mile 6.6: A 0.5-mile walking path connects the towpath to Glen Echo Park.

Mile 7.3: Pass under the 220-foot-long arch of the Cabin John Bridge, an engineering marvel of the 1850s.

Mile 12.6: Enter Widewater, a broad section of the canal that looks like a mountain lake. The going gets a bit rough for 0.25 mile, where you may have to walk your bike over rocks and boulders. To avoid this, you can cross over the canal at mile 13.5 and ride on the opposite side for a while. To get back, you'll have to carry your bike up and down several stairs on a walkway over the canal. I'd chose the stairs over the rocks, but either way you'll have to carry your bike a short distance.

Mile 15.0: Arrive at Great Falls Tavern, a hostelry built in 1831 and restored in 1942. Today the whitewashed structure houses a museum. Be sure to view the spectacular falls from the platform. From this location, looking 20 degrees to the right, you can spot an active bald eagle nest spreading out among the high branches of a sycamore. It's on the banks of a river island.

Option: The length of this ride will satisfy most cyclists, but if you want to explore the canal farther, you can ride another 7 miles to Seneca Creek. The creek is close to several old quarries from which the stone for the Smithsonian Castle was pulled. Points of interest en route include Swain's Lock, the site of an old lock keeper's house now used to rent canoes and bikes (301–299–9006) and sell snacks. After Pennyfield lock, site of the ruins of historic Tobytown, the river grows quite wide. Just up to the left, a bottomland marsh has been designated a waterfowl sanctuary. It's full of wildflowers, fish, and herons as well as ducks and geese.

The quality of the towpath surface degenerates after Seneca Creek. Although riding the entire 184-mile route (with detours and overnight stops) is a popular "once-in-a-lifetime" experience, the Georgetown–Seneca route offers years' worth of exploration. I've yet to exhaust my interest. If you would like to learn more about the canal, you might want to join a free bicycle tour led by a National Park Service ranger. Every Saturday during summer months, a group starts at 9:00 a.m. from the canal visitor center on Thomas Jefferson Street in Georgetown. The ride goes to Great Falls and takes about three hours. Bikers are on their own after that to explore as they wish and ride back. No reservations are required, but you might call to be sure the trip has not been canceled due to weather (202–653–5190).

Note: In January 1996 a major flood breached the canal and ravaged its towpath. Repairs were made, and the trail is now open. More permanent fixes are continuing, however; sections of the towpath may be under repair. Call the Chesapeake and Ohio Canal Visitor Center at (301) 767–3714 for up-to-date information.

LOCAL INFORMATION

◆ Chesapeake & Ohio Canal Visitor Center, 11710 MacArthur Boulevard, Potomac, MD 20254; (301) 767–3714; www.nps.gov/choh.
◆ D.C. Chamber of Commerce, 1213 K Street N.W., Washington, D.C. 20005; (202) 347–7201.
◆ Conference and Visitors Bureau of Montgomery County, Maryland, Inc., 11820 Parklawn Drive, Suite 380, Rockville, MD 20852; (301) 428–9702 or (800) 925–0880.
◆ Montgomery County Recreation Department, 12210 Bushey Drive, Silver Spring, MD 20902; (240) 777–6804 (general information—recording).

LOCAL EVENTS/ATTRACTIONS

◆ Glen Echo Park, 7300 MacArthur Boulevard, Glen Echo, MD 20812; (301) 492–6229; www.nps.gov/glec.

ACCOMMODATIONS

♦ Old Angler's Inn, 10801 MacArthur Boulevard, Potomac, MD 20854; (301) 299–9097.
♦ Bed & Breakfast Accommodations, P.O. Box 12011, Washington, D.C. 20005; (202) 328–3510; www.bnbaccom.com.
♦ Washington D.C. Accommodations, 2201 Wisconsin Avenue, Suite C110, Washington, D.C. 20007; (202) 289–2220 or (800) 554–2220; www.wdcahotels. com.

BIKE SHOPS

♦ Revolution Cycles, at the foot of Key Bridge, 3411 M Street N.W., Washington, D.C. 20007; (202) 965–3601.
♦ The Bicycle Pro Shop, 3403 M Street N.W., Washington, D.C. 20007; (202) 337–0311.
♦ Big Wheel Bikes, 1034 Thirty-third Street N.W., Washington, D.C. 20007; (202) 337–0254.

MAPS

♦ *ADC's Washington Area Bike Map.* Compiled by Metropolitan Washington Council of Governments. $10.95. Available at bookstores and newsstands.
♦ *D.C. Bikeways.* Series of maps published by the city. $3.00. Write to District of Columbia Office of Documents, 441 Fourth Street N.W., Suite 520, Washington, D.C. 20001; (202) 727–5090.
♦ *Maryland Bicycle Touring Map.* Free. Available from Office of Tourism Development, 45 Calvert Street, Annapolis, MD 21401.
♦ *Trails in Montgomery County Parks.* Contact Maryland–National Capital Park and Planning Commission (MNCPPC), 8787 Georgia Avenue N.W., Silver Spring, MD 20910; (301) 495–2503; www.mncppc.org.

South Arlington Ramble

T his short ramble will give you the benefit of four trails and whisk you about what is a veritable commuting trail during the week. From the starting point down by Roosevelt Island, it climbs up into Rosslyn and eastern Arlington, peaking around the East Falls Church Metro and sweeping you back down the W & OD Trail and Four-Mile Run Trail down the west side of Arlington. Hop onto the Mount Vernon Trail as it comes out of Alexandria and you're on your way back to the starting point. Along the Potomac, you can take in the sights and the tourists seeing the sights. Early in the morning and just after work, this ride is peppered with joggers, cyclists, and commuters. During the middle of the day, for the most part, you will find that you have the sunny trail to yourself.

At 25.7 square miles, Arlington is the smallest county in the United States, but it has resolved to become one of the best municipalities for cycling, with more than 75 miles of trails and on-street routes. Arlington's reputation as a cycling mecca was solidified in 1989 with the Virginia debut of the Tour duPont, America's biggest pro cycling race. Former Tour de France winner Greg LeMond and other world-class riders contested a stage of this two-week race along the George Washington Parkway.

Though the area that is now Arlington was discovered by Captain John Smith in 1607 and first mapped out as part of the District of Columbia in 1791, it remained unsettled for much longer. Small farms arrived only around 1850,

Sharing the trails in late fall

Start: Roosevelt Island parking lot

Distance: 18-mile loop

Approximate pedaling time: 2 hours

Terrain and surface: Rolling; excellent off-road trail with center stripe, boardwalk, ramps, and bridges

Things to see: "Contemporary urban development," wildflower meadow, bird sanctuary, pretty neighborhoods, creek, and Potomac shores

Traffic and hazards: None

Facilities: Rest rooms, parks, and water fountains en route

Getting there: From Washington, cross Roosevelt Bridge and turn north onto George Washington Parkway. In 0.5 mile turn into Roosevelt Island parking lot. From Alexandria, north on George Washington Parkway. By Metro, take Blue or Orange Line to Rosslyn; ride toward Key Bridge and pick up bike route before crossing.

and government workers in search of suburbs to settle came around 1910. Farms and log cabins could be found within its boundaries into the twentieth century. Well before all that, the original inhabitants were probably the Doegs and Necostins of the Algonquin tribes. Today's Arlington is a rapidly developing area with about 140,000 residents. Charming and historic bungalow neighborhoods stand cheek by jowl with new high-rises and highways.

This trip, which uses sections for four bike paths, begins at Theodore Roosevelt Island, a park of natural beauty, all too close to Rosslyn, the high-rise district (and home of *USA Today*). A trip down the interstate will take you into the heart of the county.

Along with parts of Route 70 in Colorado, this section of Interstate 66 through Arlington is one of the few interstate highways in the United States that not only allows but encourages cycling. Like its Rocky Mountain counterpart, Interstate 66 features a well-thought-out multiuse trail made possible by spectacular engineering. The path soars well above the roadbed on buff-colored concrete barriers that also muffle road noise from the adjoining neighborhoods and crisscrosses the four-lane road on high ramps and bridges. The grades are surprisingly steep and frequent. It's a trip through a manufactured mountain range that I call the Concrete Cotswolds.

That said, the route (also known officially as the Custis Memorial Trail) is darned handy. Its many direct connections include Key Bridge into Georgetown, the Theodore Roosevelt Island Pedestrian/Bicycle Bridge leading to the Mount Vernon Trail, the W & OD Trail, and the Four-Mile Run Trail. It's also the middle link for an uninterrupted 64-mile off-road ride through northern Virginia (which can be extended by crossing into Washington or Maryland).

Moreover, connections to at least a dozen neighborhoods and commercial areas allow residents to commute or shop without a car. The signs on the trail point you exactly where you're going; for a change, they're at least as good as the road signs.

All this came about as a result of a twenty-five-year battle to build Interstate 66, originally conceived as an eight-lane superhighway. Neighborhood groups sued to save their homes and trees, while the highway engineers compromised by cutting back on auto lanes, adding a median for Metrorail, planning parks and sound barriers, and designing this impressive bike byway. Opposition never dissolved entirely, but the road did get built.

About the only thing lacking along Interstate 66 is scenery. Mostly you see banal high-rises, zooming autos, and plastic-looking plantings. It does, however, get you to where you're going: the much more bucolic Four-Mile Run Trail, which meets at a wildflower meadow at Interstate 66 near the Beltway and the East Falls Church Metrorail station.

Four-Mile Run forms the second side of a triangular route around Arlington. The creek serves as the natural border between Arlington County and Alexandria City. Close by its southern section, you can find an original D.C. boundary marker, an old quarry, a meadow preserve, and the remains of an old bungalow-and-cottage neighborhood that was divided by highway construction. The path is broad and smooth and is bisected by a dotted yellow line, which should be standard equipment on all trails. Head along the creek's south bank into Bon Air Park, where there is a rose garden well worth seeing in season.

Continue through a valley into Glen Carlyn Park, which blooms with mountain laurel, dogwood, and azalea in spring. A waterfall marks the location of an old mill. Excursion steam trains once stopped here to pick up water for their locomotives. This is Arlington's own fall line, signifying the end of the coastal plain and the commencement of the Piedmont Plateau. George Washington once surveyed the site. Look for a historical marker. More history: Near South Fourth Street, just off the trail, is the 1742 Ball-Sellers House, once owned by George Washington's tailor. The W & OD bike path and Four-Mile Run Trail merge periodically or run parallel at this point.

After crossing under Arlington Boulevard, the route bifurcates into low and high roads. The high road offers vistas, but the low road (actually part of the W & OD Trail) is much safer. At Columbia Pike, the W & OD Trail takes the high road over the street; follow the Four-Mile Run bike path under this busy street. After passing through a broad forest, you exit not into a meadow but into a very urban area, replete with a fording of Interstate 395.

Adjacent to 395 is Shirlington Village, a former strip shopping mall that has been reconstituted as a "neotraditional" development that's supposed to recall an old-fashioned brick-lined Main Street. It's a place to stroll or have an ice cream cone, and there's a bike shop on the main drag. Pick up the trail again to cross Interstate 395, through neighborhood streets to the Anderson bike path. This parallels Four-Mile Run to where it drains into the Potomac, near a rail

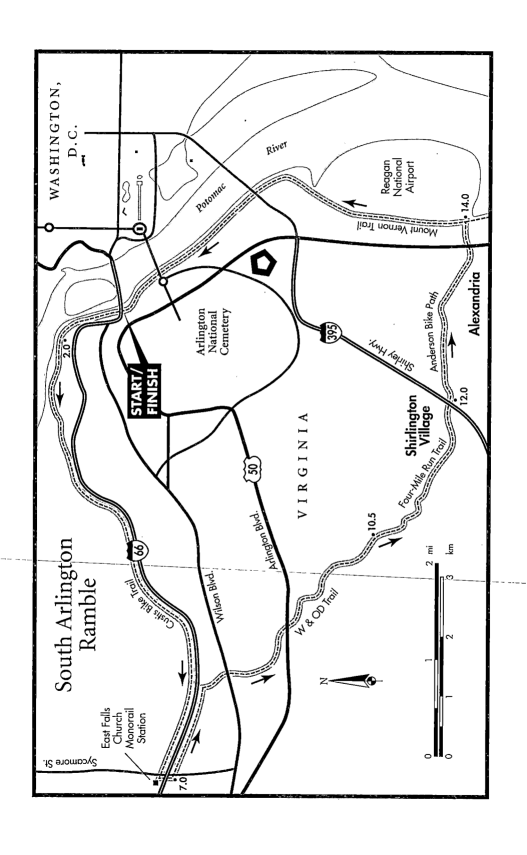

South Arlington Ramble

WASHINGTON, D.C.

Potomac River

Reagan National Airport

Mount Vernon Trail

• 14.0

Arlington National Cemetery

START/ FINISH

2.0

395

Shirley Hwy.

Anderson Bike Path

Alexandria

• 12.0

VIRGINIA

Shirlington Village

Four-Mile Run Trail

50

Arlington Blvd.

Wilson Blvd.

• 10.5

W & OD Trail

66

Custis Bike Trail

East Falls Church Monorail Station

Sycamore St.

• 7.0

N

2 mi
km

0   1   2
0   1   2   3

0.0 From parking lot, north on bike path and up biker/hiker bridge over George Washington Parkway.

2.0 Stay on bike path; cross Fort Meyer Drive at Key Bridge. Follow bike path on sidewalk next to Lee Highway. Custis Bike Trail begins here, behind a concrete sound barrier. Head west for 5 miles on trail.

7.0 Right at T intersection, remaining on Custis Bike Trail. In less than 0.1 mile, left at second T intersection onto W & OD Bike Trail heading east. (To head to East Falls Church Metrorail station, turn right onto W & OD Trail and head 1 mile to East Falls Church Park, then right on North Roosevelt.) On W & OD Trail, head southwest under Wilson and Arlington Boulevards and Walter Reed Drive.

10.5 At Columbia Pike, W & OD and Four-Mile Run Bike Trails split. Bear right onto Four-Mile Run Trail under Columbia Pike.

12.0 Near Interstate 395, right onto South Randolph Street and left onto South Twenty-eighth Street. Follow bike-path signs onto sidewalk on north side of street, then around corner to pedestrian overpass of Shirley Highway (395).

12.5 Left onto Custis Road.

13.0 Left onto West Glebe Road. Use sidewalk to reach South Glebe Road, which leads to Wayne F. Anderson Bike Path (busy and poorly marked).

13.8 Follow sidewalk over Route 1 to passage under railroad tracks leading to Mount Vernon Trail.

14.0 Left onto Mount Vernon Trail. Follow signs to Rosslyn and take path under Memorial Bridge (rather than bearing left, which will divert you across the George Washington Parkway toward Arlington Cemetery—see Ride 1). Right into parking lot.

yard and Reagan National Airport. At this transportation nexus, turn left onto the Mount Vernon Trail, which takes you safely back to Roosevelt Island.

LOCAL INFORMATION

♦ Arlington Chamber of Commerce, 2009 Fourteenth Street, North, Suite 111, Arlington, VA 22201; (703) 525–2400.
♦ Arlington Convention and Visitors Service, 1100 North Glebe Road, Suite 1500, Arlington, VA 22201; (703) 228–0888 or (800) 677–6267.

LOCAL EVENTS/ATTRACTIONS

♦ Contact the Arlington Convention and Visitors Service.

ACCOMMODATIONS

♦ Best Western Key Bridge, 1850 North Fort Myer Drive, Arlington, VA; 22209; (703) 522–0400 or (800) KEY–BRIDGE.

BIKE SHOPS

♦ Revolution Cycles, 2731 Wilson Boulevard Arlington, VA 22201; (703) 312–0007.

MAPS

♦ *W & OD R.R. Regional Park Trail Guide.* $5.95. Contact Northern Virginia Regional Park Authority, 5400 Ox Road, Fairfax Station, VA 22039; (703) 352–5900. Also available from the W & OD Trail office at (703) 729–0596 and some bike shops.

♦ *Arlington, Virginia, Bikeway Map and Guide.* Published by the Arlington County Department of Public Works. Free. Contact Public Works Planning Division, No. 1 Court House Plaza, 2100 North Clarendon Boulevard, Arlington, VA 22201; (703) 228–3681.

♦ *Virginia Atlas and Gazetteer.* Published by DeLorme Mapping Company. Includes topographic maps, hike/bike trails, canoeing areas. $12.95. Available at bookstores.

♦ *ADC's Washington Area Bike Map.* Compiled by Metropolitan Washington Council of Governments. $10.95. Available at bookstores and newsstands.

♦ *D.C. Bikeways.* Series of maps published by the city. $3.00. Write to District of Columbia Office of Documents, 441 Fourth Street N.W., Suite 520, Washington, D.C. 20001; (202) 727–5090.

North Arlington Ramble

Y ou live in North Arlington and are looking for a short, fun ride you can fit into a busy schedule. Or you'd like to know an easy way across Chain Bridge so you can follow the C & O towpath into Georgetown for brunch, out to Great Falls for a picnic, or even to Bethesda via the Capital Crescent Trail. Or maybe you live on the Maryland side of the Potomac and would like to explore a little bit of Arlington.

Here's a convenient ride that loops around Arlington's suburban highlands, perched high above the Potomac River in the county's northern corner. It connects a few very ridable artery roads with a streamside bike path to form a simple 10-mile loop.

Start at Potomac Overlook Regional Park, which features tennis courts, playing fields, a nature center, and a picnic area.

Exit the park via Marcy Road and turn right onto Military Road. At the bottom of the hill, where the road narrows to two lanes, turn left to cross Military Road (carefully!) and follow the bike path that leads off into the woods. The path alternates between hard-packed dirt and pavement as it winds

Riding west on the bike path

Idyllic homes surrounded by old trees make the tour of North Arlington peaceful and relaxing.

its way up this narrow, wooded watershed.

Emerge from the trees and return to regular roads across from Marymount College. Turn left onto North Twenty-eighth Street, and then immediately right onto Yorktown Boulevard. Following a few up-and-down blocks through this well-kept neighborhood, turn right onto George Mason Drive. Cars would face a dead end here, but you can continue straight onto the short section of bike path that crosses a stream and connects to another stretch of George Mason Drive. Ride on for a few more blocks, then turn right onto Williamsburg Boulevard.

Williamsburg, following a short steep hill, ends at a stoplight. Turn left here onto North Glebe Road, Route 120, which leads to Chain Bridge. Rather than follow this road all the way to the river, turn right onto Old Glebe Road at the big white church. This original route to the river passes by some nice, older cottages before connecting with Military Road.

On your right is the new Ethan Allen Park, the former site of one of many defensive positions ringing Washington during the Civil War. Built by troops from Vermont, the fort was named for Vermont's famous Revolutionary War commander. An exhibit provides a visual display of the ring of forts which saw action.

Turn right onto Military to return to Marcy Road. On the way, stop and explore Gulf Branch Nature Center. You can park your bikes here and follow a narrow ravine trail down to the shore of the Potomac. This is a favorite spot for fishing or for just viewing the river up close.

For views from a higher vantage point, explore Potomac Overlook Park's network of short trails. But not by bike—Arlington is cyclist-friendly, as this ride will have shown, but these trails are for hikers only.

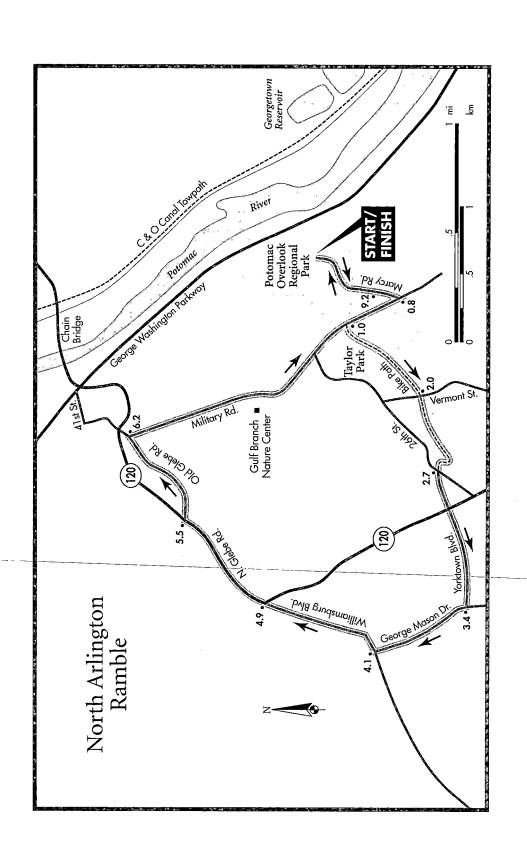

North Arlington Ramble

Georgetown
Reservoir

C & O Canal Towpath

River

Potomac

Chain
Bridge

George Washington Parkway

Potomac
Overlook
Regional
Park

**START/
FINISH**

Marcy Rd.

9.2

0.8

1.0

Taylor
Park

Bike Path

2.0

Vermont St.

41st St.

6.2

Old Glebe Rd.

Military Rd.

Gulf Branch
Nature Center ■

26th St.

2.7

120

5.5

N. Glebe Rd.

120

Yorktown Blvd.

Williamsburg Blvd.

4.9

George Mason Dr.

3.4

4.1

N

1 mi

km

.5

1

.5

0

0

0.0 Exit Potomac Overlook Regional Park on Marcy Road.

0.8 Right onto Military Road.

1.0 At bottom of long hill, where Military narrows to two lanes, dismount and walk your bike across Military. Here, at Taylor Park, follow a narrow bike path into the woods.

2.0 Continue on bike path as it crosses North Vernon and Vermont Streets.

2.7 Left onto North Twenty-sixth Street, directly across from Marymount College, at the bike path's end. Immediate right onto Yorktown Boulevard, which passes beneath North Glebe Road.

3.4 Right onto George Mason Drive. At dead end, continue straight onto short bike path leading to separate section of George Mason.

4.1 Right onto Williamsburg Boulevard.

4.9 Left onto North Glebe Road (Route 120) at traffic light.

5.5 Right onto Old Glebe Road at white church.   )

6.2 Right onto Military Road. (Or, to access Chain Bridge, continue straight onto the overpass and follow the directions under Option, below.)

9.2 Left onto Marcy Road to start/finish at Potomac Overlook Regional Park.

Option: To connect this ride with the C & O Canal towpath or Capital Crescent Trail via Chain Bridge, follow Old Glebe Road straight onto the overpass over North Glebe instead of turning right onto Military Road. Bear right on the other side, then turn left onto North Randolph Street. Look for a bike-path entrance on the right—it's next to a log-cabin-style house—and follow it down a steep stretch to North Forty-first Street and a small parking area. Follow the marked bike lane through a busy intersection and directly onto the protected sidewalk across the bridge. On the Maryland side of the bridge, there's a hiker/biker ramp providing direct access to the canal towpath. Turn left to head in the direction of Great Falls, or right to reach Georgetown or the Capital Crescent Trail.

LOCAL INFORMATION

♦ Arlington Chamber of Commerce, 2009 Fourteenth Street North, Suite 111, Arlington, VA 22201; (703) 525–2400.

♦ Arlington Convention and Visitors Service, 1100 North Glebe Road, Suite 1500, Arlington, VA 22201; (703) 228–0888 or (800) 677–6267.

LOCAL EVENTS/ATTRACTIONS

♦ Contact the Arlington Convention and Visitors Service.

ACCOMMODATIONS

♦ Best Western Key Bridge, 1850 North Fort Myer Drive, Arlington, VA 22209; (703) 522–0400 or (800) KEY–BRIDGE.

BIKE SHOPS

♦ Revolution Cycles, 2731 Wilson Boulevard, Arlington, VA 22201; (703) 312–0007.

MAPS

♦ *W & OD R.R. Regional Park Trail Guide.* $5.95. Contact Northern Virginia Regional Park Authority, 5400 Ox Road, Fairfax Station, VA 22039; (703) 352–5900. Also available from the W & OD Trail office at (703) 729–0596 and some bike shops.

♦ *Arlington, Virginia, Bikeway Map and Guide.* Published by the Arlington County Department of Public Works. Free. Contact Public Works Planning Division, No. 1 Court House Plaza, 2100 North Clarendon Boulevard, Arlington, VA 22201; (703) 228–3681.

♦ *Virginia Atlas and Gazetteer.* Published by DeLorme Mapping Company. Includes topographic maps, hike/bike trails, canoeing area. $12.95. Available at bookstores.

♦ *ADC's Washington Area Bike Map.* Compiled by Metropolitan Washington Council of Governments. $10.95. Available at bookstores and newsstands.

♦ *D.C. Bikeways.* Series of maps published by the city. $3.00. Write to District of Columbia Office of Documents, 441 Fourth Street N.W., Suite 520, Washington, D.C. 20001; (202) 727–5090.

Neighborhoods of
Northwest D.C. Ramble

H ere's a ride that takes you through a part of Washington that tourists rarely see—the places beyond the monuments where people actually live. The route meanders through row-house neighborhoods both historic and of more recent vintage. Catch a bit of Takoma Park's New Age funk before visiting the site where the South almost won the Civil War, then see one of the capital's premier upper-middle-class neighborhoods before swinging through Rock Creek Park to urbane Dupont Circle.

This route is for a special breed of rider—the city biker. These intrepid pedalers don't mind dressing from head to toe in canary yellow, painting their helmets blaze orange, installing expensive puncture-proof tubes, or occasionally sharing an 8-foot-wide street with an 8-foot-wide bus. They seem to enjoy themselves even while carrying locks as heavy as their bike frames and stopping for lights every 2 blocks. The rewards are seeing the urban fabric at a range close enough to explore crooked streets, read historical markers, and discover neighborhood haunts.

Some people will never know these pleasures. Cowed by traffic and poor road maintenance, they stick to bike paths and country lanes. Basically, they're exhibiting good common sense, but I still think they're missing out. Try this ride on a Sunday morning, when traffic is at a minimum. Remember to bring along extra tubes, coins for pay phones, and, ideally, a buddy for this and other urban rides described in this book.

Start: Logan Circle

Distance: 13-mile loop

Approximate pedaling time: 2 hours

Terrain and surface: Hilly; city roads, potholes and all

Things to see: Historic Logan Circle, rowhouse neighborhoods, Fort Stevens, Takoma Park, Gold Coast, lower Rock Creek Park, Dupont Circle

Traffic and hazards: This is a heavily traveled route with a lot of congestion. There are city roads with potholes, construction zones—the works!

Facilities: Rest rooms and food along the route

Option: Trip to downtown Takoma Park farmers' market

Getting there: From Dupont Circle Metro, take Dupont Circle exit and cross the circle to P Street heading east. Ride 6 blocks to Logan Circle. From downtown, take Thirteenth Street north from Pennsylvania Avenue. From Capitol Hill, take Massachusetts Avenue west to Thirteenth Street and turn right.

Start at historic Logan Circle, named for the Civil War general John A. Logan. The Civil War was the neighborhood's heyday. Gilded Age Washingtonians built preposterously large Victorian houses featuring turrets, finials, widow's walks, and any other architectural doodads they could think of. The remarkable thing is that the circle and its surrounding blocks have remained intact, even thrived with renovation in recent years. The circle itself was recently restored when two extra traffic lanes were removed in favor of grass and shrubs.

Head north up a steep hill that is Thirteenth Street. You're in the midst of another architecturally interesting, but fairly gritty, neighborhood (Columbia Heights), so be careful. At the heights, pass the magnificent edifice of Cardozo High, home to a famous marching band, and keep your eyes peeled for a bike-route sign pointing to Takoma Park via Third Street.

The scene remains urban but loses some of its grit in favor of green, for the houses of the Brightwood area are carefully tended and are surrounded by small lawns, azaleas, and evergreens. A former farming community that was developed with row houses in the early twentieth century, it's the type of place where people set up a transistor radio on the front porch to listen to a ball game while cutting the grass with an old push mower.

The ride heads due north across short hills on straight, quiet streets. Near the apex of the city of Washington, take a short detour to the area's first real suburb, Takoma Park, Maryland. Built after 1883 to provide inexpensive housing connected to the city by rail and streetcar, Takoma Park today is an amalgamation of many things: grand Queen Anne houses and tiny bungalows; tie-dyed types who never stopped being hippies and young lawyers; and quiet suburban living and city amenities. A good reason to stop here is the food. On Sundays a farmers' market fills part of Carroll Avenue, and there are good cafes and bakeries nearby as well. For now, at least, Takoma Park is also a suburb without malls. In 1995 development plans that would change that distinction began to make headway with the local government. Brick-lined Carroll Avenue is a real Main Street, complete with a clock tower and a pharmacy run by a gentleman everyone calls "Doc."

On the way back into town, stop at reconstructed Fort Stevens to peer over the same battlements where President Lincoln nervously watched the troops of Confederate general Jubal Early advance on the underdefended capital in 1864. Bullets whizzed by Abe's stovepipe hat until Lieutenant Colonel Oliver Wendell Holmes supposedly barked, "Get down, you fool!" Early was soon repelled, however. Today the site is mostly grass, with only a few cannons, but a little imagination reconstructs the scene.

Though heading south toward the city center, you will soon leave urbanized areas behind. Colorado and Blagden Avenues cut diagonally across the street grid through the Gold Coast, a wealthy neighborhood with large Tudor houses. You will be coasting here, as the grades are all downhill. Soon you will arrive via Carter Barron Amphitheatre at Pierce Mill in Rock Creek Park. Take the Rock Creek Park bike path south and exit at Dupont Circle, the most cosmopolitan neighborhood in Washington. There are dozens of embassies, historic houses, movie theaters, art galleries, and bookshops in this historic district. After exploring the area on foot, you can either ride the 6 blocks east back to Logan Circle or jump on Metrorail's Red Line.

LOCAL INFORMATION

♦ D.C. Chamber of Commerce, 1213 K Street N.W., Washington, DC 20005; (202) 347–7201.

LOCAL EVENTS/ATTRACTIONS

♦ Rock Creek Park, Washington, D.C.; www.nps.gov. Luckily for Washingtonians, in 1890 Congress prevented this 1,800-acre green valley that cuts a swathe from Georgetown north through the city to the Maryland state line from becoming the unofficial city dump. Today this tranquil urban valley is a haven for bikers, joggers, and picnickers. It is a place where people can enjoy themselves, sitting quietly under the shade trees along the banks of the creek, cooking over a barbecue grill, or enjoying the sight and fragrance of the daffodils and other flowers that bloom here each spring.
♦ Rock Creek Park Nature Center & Planetarium, 5200 Glover Road N.W., Washington, D.C.; (202) 426–6829. A spot where you can see live and mounted wildlife displays, environmental exhibits, and planetarium shows, as well as participate in guided nature walks. For horseback-riding lessons, visit the Horse Centre off Military Road at 5100 Glover Road N.W. Call (202) 362–0117.

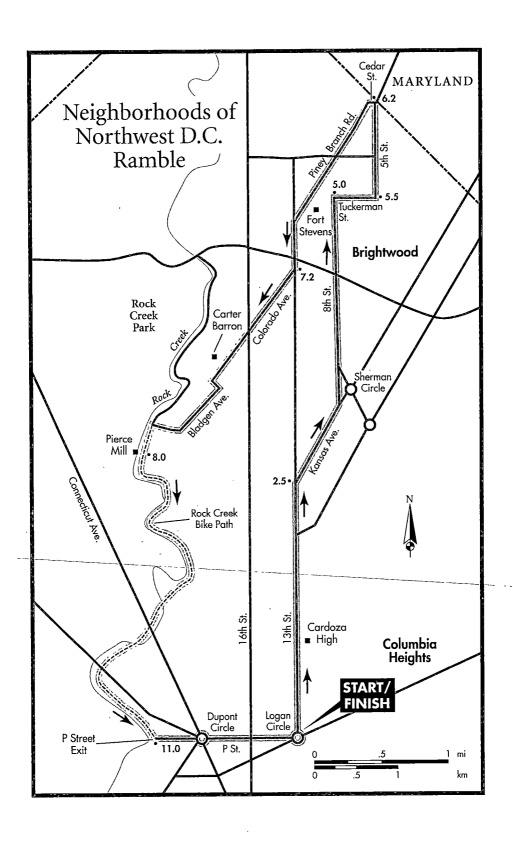

Neighborhoods of Northwest D.C. Ramble

Cedar St.

MARYLAND

• 6.2

Piney Branch Rd.

5th St.

5.0 •

• 5.5

Tuckerman St.

■ Fort Stevens

Brightwood

• 7.2

8th St.

Colorado Ave.

Rock Creek Park

Carter Barron

Creek

Rock

Sherman Circle

Bladgen Ave.

Pierce Mill ■ • 8.0

Kansas Ave.

2.5 •

Connecticut Ave.

Rock Creek Bike Path

N

16th St.

13th St.

Cardoza ■ High

Columbia Heights

START/ FINISH

Dupont Circle

Logan Circle

P Street Exit

• 11.0

P St.

| 0 | | .5 | | 1 mi |
| 0 | .5 | | 1 | km |

0.0 Start at Logan Circle at the intersection of Vermont and Rhode Island Avenues and Thirteenth Street N.W. Head north about 25 blocks on Thirteenth Street.

2.5 Watch for sign pointing to bike route to Takoma Park. Soft right onto Kansas Avenue.

3.0 Left at Eighth Street to enter Brightwood neighborhood.

5.0 In about 20 blocks, right onto Tuckerman Street.

5.5 In 4 blocks, left onto Fifth Street N.W.

6.2 Ride 5 blocks to Cedar Street N.W. To visit Takoma Park, Maryland, turn right onto Cedar, which turns into Carroll Avenue (main street) after crossing under railroad tracks. To return to downtown D.C., turn left onto Cedar and left onto Piney Branch Road.

6.9 Visit Fort Stevens (on left near Quackenbos Street).

7.2 Continue on Piney Branch (becomes Thirteenth Street) to Colorado Avenue (signed bike route). Turn right.

7.3 At Fourteenth Street, quick left and right to remain on Colorado Avenue.

7.6 Left at Seventeenth Street.

7.7 In 2 short blocks, right onto Blagden Avenue. Take Blagden Avenue to Beach Drive in Rock Creek Park.

7.9 Turn right onto Beach Drive, then immediately left onto Broad Branch.

8.0 Left through small parking lot to Pierce Mill. At Pierce Mill, join Rock Creek Bike Path heading south.

11.0 In about 3 miles, take parkway exit marked for Dupont Circle. At top of exit ramp, right onto P Street. Left onto Twentieth Street to reach Dupont Circle Metro station (bike racks available) or continue around Dupont Circle and eastward on P Street to return to Logan Circle.

13.0 Arrive at Logan Circle.

ACCOMMODATIONS

♦ Bed & Breakfast Accommodations, P.O. Box 12011, Washington, D.C. 20005; (202) 328–3510; www.bnbaccom.com.

♦ Washington D.C. Accommodations, 2201 Wisconsin Avenue, Suite C110, Washington, D.C. 20007; (202) 289–2220 or (800) 554–2220; www.wdca hotels.com.

♦ Washington Courtyard by Marriott, 1900 Connecticut Avenue N.W., Washington, D.C. 20009; (202) 332–9300; www.courtyard.com.

BIKE SHOPS

♦ Revolution Cycles, at the foot of Key Bridge, 3411 M Street N.W., Washington, D.C.; (202) 965–3601.
♦ The Bicycle Pro Shop, 3403 M Street N.W., Washington, D.C. 20007; (202) 337–0311.
♦ Big Wheel Bikes, 1034 Thirty-third Street N.W., Washington, D.C.; (202) 337–0254.

MAPS

♦ *ADC's Washington Area Bike Map.* Compiled by Metropolitan Washington Council of Governments. $10.95. Available at bookstores and newsstands.
♦ *D.C. Bikeways.* Series of maps published by the city. $3.00. Write to District of Columbia Office of Documents, 441 Fourth Street N.W., Suite 520, Washington, D.C. 20001; (202) 727–5090.

Dupont—Georgetown— Cleveland Park Ramble

I *f you could only block out the traffic, this would be the city ride that would make you forget you're in the city, for these are both Washington's leafiest and most affluent neighborhoods, each with its own character. Georgetown, which existed as a thriving port long before the District of Columbia was conceived, has its brick sidewalks, cobblestone streets, and absurdly narrow row houses; Dupont Circle, its bistro and bookstore nightlife; Cleveland Park, its rambling wooden houses and big shade trees; and Embassy Row, its mansions that could have been plucked from Gatsby's North Shore. A stop along the way, the National Cathedral, features rolling grounds punctuated by flowering trees, and an herb garden that would be the envy of its English progenitors.*

To avoid some of the heavy traffic, this ride would be best early Saturday morning. Keep in mind that parking is very sparse and limited to two hours. The ride should be taken at a very slow pace to enjoy views of gardens and stop to read plaques. Start at the Q Street entrance to the Dupont Circle Metro. The neighborhood's nerve center across the street is Kramer Books & Afterwords Cafe, which serves up spinach quiche with its Spinoza. After fortifying body and mind, head for P Street, a lively corridor of restaurants, boutiques, and coffeehouses. It's hard to believe that before 1873 this urbane row was a humble creek surrounded by farmland. Within thirty years this was the most fashionable address in Washington, by 1950 a slum, and now again pricey and restored.

Cross the 1914 Buffalo Bridge to Q Street for an introduction to some of Georgetown's finer houses. Farther up Q Street is Dumbarton Oaks, a palatial estate owned by Harvard University and open to the public for limited hours. Its attractions include a fantastic formal garden and a museum (designed by Philip Johnson) of pre-Columbian art. Cross Wisconsin Avenue, one of Washington's busiest shopping streets, and ride through more blocks of ornate old houses until Q Street ends.

After pedaling uphill and fighting Wisconsin Avenue traffic, you arrive some 400 feet above the level of the Potomac. The climb will be rewarded by a visit to one of the world's largest churches, the Washington Cathedral (National Cathedral). From some angles on the Potomac's south bank, the limestone towers of this Gothic wonder actually loom over the Capitol dome. The cathedral was undertaken in 1907 using medieval construction methods and wasn't completed until 1990. There are some modern details, such as stained-glass windows commemorating the moon landing, and a gargoyle that parodies a modern lawyer on the run. There's an observation deck in one of three towers, a gift shop, a brass-rubbing center, and a small commercial greenhouse.

The cathedral borders Cleveland Park, Washington's newest historic district and unofficial Volvo capital of the free world. Its residents tend to be former free spirits now plugging through the upper echelons of journalism and law. The oldest house here dates from 1780. According to historian Kathleen Sinclair Wood, the area's frame houses and wraparound porches are "reminiscent of small-town America . . . within minutes of central Washington."

Exit Cleveland Park via busy Thirty-fourth Street to Massachusetts Avenue. As you turn left, the vice president's residence since 1977, a white turreted structure on the grounds of the U.S. Naval Observatory, is visible beyond a fence on the right. (Careful: The intersection sees more bike accidents than any other in the city.) Straight ahead is the Naval Observatory itself, with its 125-year-old telescope, used to discover the moons of Mars in 1877, and the Master Clock of the United States, the world's most accurate timepiece.

The scenery gets much more grandiose as you head down Massachusetts Avenue. You pass the embassies of Britain, Brazil, Japan, and Turkey. There are formal gardens, specimen trees, and a statue of Winston Churchill flashing V-for-victory. The latest addition to this diplomatic corridor is a memorial to poet-philosopher Kahlil Gibran. Though lined by stately linden trees, this is not the most inspiring bicycling territory—you ride on a sidewalk on a street clogged with traffic—but it is a fitting end to a tour of Washington at its most cultivated.

LOCAL INFORMATION

♦ D.C. Chamber of Commerce, 1213 K Street N.W., Washington, D.C. 20005; (202) 347–7201.

LOCAL EVENTS/ATTRACTIONS

♦ Rock Creek Park, Washington, D.C.; www.nps.gov. Luckily for Washingtonians, in 1890 Congress prevented this 1,800-acre green valley that cuts a swathe from Georgetown north through the city to the Maryland state line from becoming the unofficial city dump. Today this tranquil urban valley is a haven for bikers, joggers, and picnickers. It is a place where people can enjoy themselves, sitting quietly under the shade trees along the banks of the creek, cooking over a barbecue grill, or enjoying the sight and fragrance of the daffodils and other flowers that bloom here each spring.
♦ Rock Creek Park Nature Center & Planetarium, 5200 Glover Road N.W., Washington, D.C.; (202) 426–6829. A spot where you can see live and mounted wildlife displays, environmental exhibits, and planetarium shows, as well as participate in guided nature walks. For horseback-riding lessons, visit the Horse Centre off Military Road at 5100 Glover Road N.W. Call (202) 362–0117.

ACCOMMODATIONS

♦ Bed & Breakfast Accommodations, P.O. Box 12011, Washington, D.C. 20005; (202) 328–3510; www.bnbaccom.com.
♦ Washington D.C. Accommodations, 2201 Wisconsin Avenue, Suite C110, Washington, D.C. 20007; (202) 289–2220 or (800) 554–2220; www.wdcahotels.com.
♦ Washington Courtyard by Marriott, 1900 Connecticut Avenue N.W., Washington, D.C. 20009; (202) 332–9300; www.courtyard.com.

BIKE SHOPS

♦ Revolution Cycles, at the foot of Key Bridge, 3411 M Street N.W., Washington, D.C. 20007; (202) 965–3601.

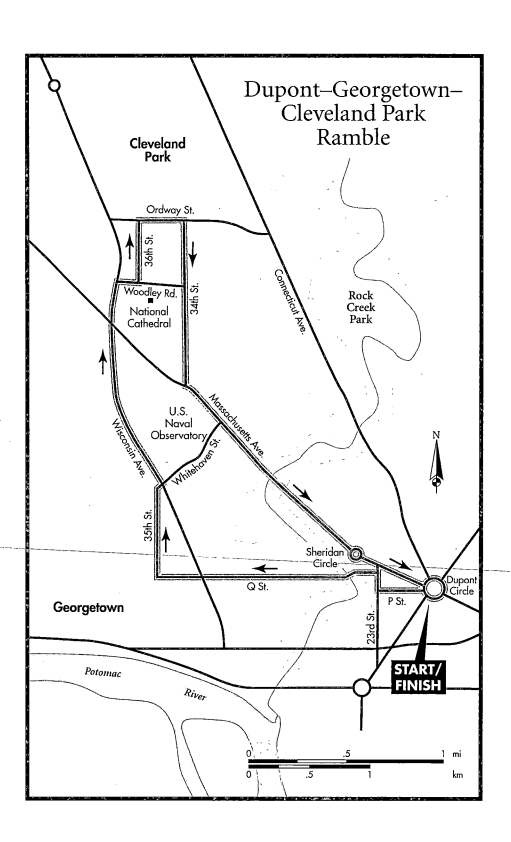

Dupont–Georgetown–Cleveland Park Ramble

Cleveland
Park

Ordway St.

36th St.

Woodley Rd.

National
Cathedral

34th St.

Connecticut Ave.

Rock
Creek
Park

Massachusetts Ave.

U.S.
Naval
Observatory

Wisconsin Ave.

Whitehaven St.

N

35th St.

Sheridan
Circle

Q St.

Dupont
Circle

P St.

23rd St.

Georgetown

Potomac

River

START/
FINISH

0   .5   1 mi

0   .5   1 km

Note: Use blocks and features to navigate instead of miles.
- From Q Street entrance to Dupont Circle Metro, head south on Twentieth Street 2 blocks to P Street. Turn right.
- In 3 blocks, right onto Twenty-third Street and immediately left onto Q Street.
- Cross Wisconsin Avenue in Georgetown; jog right and then left onto Q Street again.
- Right onto Thirty-fifth Street.
- Right onto Whitehaven Street.
- Left onto Wisconsin Avenue (heavy traffic for 10 blocks).
- Right through arched entrance to National Cathedral grounds.
- Exit cathedral grounds and turn right onto Woodley Road.
- Left onto Thirty-sixth Street in Cleveland Park.
- In 5 blocks, right onto Ordway Street.
- In 2 blocks, right onto Thirty-fourth Street (heavy traffic).
- In about 7 blocks, left onto Massachusetts Avenue (bike route on sidewalk).
- Stay on sidewalk to Sheridan Circle at Twenty-third Street.
- Go around circle to stay on Massachusetts. In 2 blocks, left onto Q Street.
- Return to Dupont Circle Metro.

- The Bicycle Pro Shop, 3403 M Street N.W., Washington, D.C. 20007; (202) 337–0311.
- Big Wheel Bikes, 1034 Thirty-third Street N.W., Washington, D.C 20007; (202) 337–0254.

MAPS

- *ADC's Washington Area Bike Map.* Compiled by Metropolitan Washington Council of Governments. $10.95. Available at bookstores and newsstands.
- *D.C. Bikeways.* Series of maps published by the city. $3.00. Write to District of Columbia Office of Documents, 441 Fourth Street N.W., Suite 520, Washington, D.C. 20001; (202) 727–5090.

Prince William Forest
Park Ramble

T his is a simple, 13-mile ride that's great for getting into shape for longer rides. It includes a 6-mile loop you can ride a few times for a longer workout. You can even switch modes by bringing mountain bikes to ride the 20 miles of fire roads through the dense forest of this unusual national park.

Before setting out, keep in mind that a few of the fire roads are closed to bikes. Check with the ranger before revving up the stump-jumper. He or she will give you a map showing approved routes. When this was written, routes *not* recommended for biking included the North Orenda Road and Old Pyrite Road. A park spokesperson also warned bikers against riding on the 35 miles of hiking trails. "Our rangers are ready to nab 'em," she said.

There's excellent camping (both tents and trailer-hook-ups) should you wish to stay over to spend a second day hiking. Small tent sites are available on a first-come, first-served basis and cost $10. Cabins and larger tent sites can be reserved; call (703) 221–4706 for information. Large groups can stay in one of five rustic camps (accommodating twenty-five to forty campers for $30 a night) built by the Civilian Conservation Corps (CCC) in the 1930s. The young construction workers milled their wood on site from fallen trees. They were paid $1.00 a day. With unemployment near 25 percent nationally, there were plenty of takers. They also built lakes near each site. Today these rough-hewn cabins, surrounded by forest and built of shingle, iron, and stone, are listed on the National Register of Historic Places.

Originally named Chopawamsic ("by the separation of the outlet"), the 16,000-acre park is a great place to relive history or to study natural history.

Even cyclists may spot a wild turkey or white-tailed deer or wend along the edge of a meadow or a stand of Virginia pine.

The park is also an example of environmental restoration. When founded by Scotsmen in the 1700s, this area was second only to New York among New World ports. By the next century pyrite mining had become the area's economic base. Sulfur was extracted from this fool's gold and refined for industrial uses. But by 1933 the centuries of mining and farming had exhausted the land. Siltation clogged Quantico Creek and consigned Dumfries Harbor to oblivion. The federal government bought 17,000 acres and ultimately directed that it be rehabilitated as wilderness. The CCC was

Scenic Drive

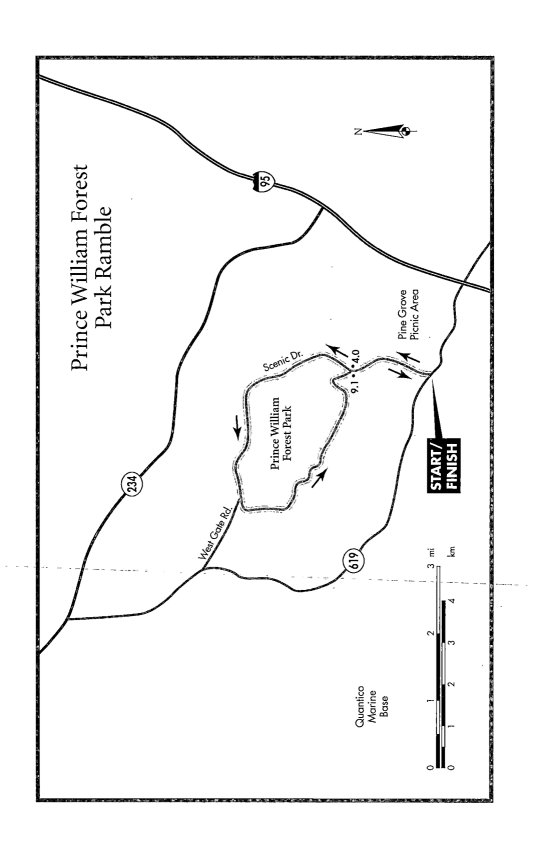

Prince William Forest Park Ramble

N

95

234

West Gate Rd.

Scenic Dr.

Prince William Forest Park

9.1 • • 4.0

Pine Grove Picnic Area

START/ FINISH

619

Quantico Marine Base

0   1   2   3 mi

0   1   2   3   4 km

0.0   From Pine Grove Picnic Area, just off Route 619, right toward park entrance.
4.0   Right onto Scenic Drive. Continue counterclockwise on Scenic Drive. Camping and rest rooms available about halfway through loop.
9.1   Turn right to head toward park exit.
13.0 Left into Pine Grove Picnic Area.

assigned to the job, and the labor was imported from tent camps right in Washington. In 1948 Prince William Forest Park was born with another social purpose: to provide inner-city youth with camping facilities. The park is still available to serve that function.

Where once were barren fields are now eighty-nine species of shrubs and trees, including hickory, beech, and mountain laurel. Bisected by many streams and paths, the park looks like a piece of nature preserved in its pristine state. The new-growth forest is home to beavers, red foxes, copperhead snakes, and the occasional bald eagle. But there are also remnants of civilization: foundations, orchards, cemeteries, and remains of the old pyrite mine.

The park's function of harboring Prince William County's open space becomes increasingly important as development fans out from Washington with accelerating speed. Right now, the park offers one of the few on-road rides in this book where I can guarantee light traffic and uncluttered scenery. There is a small price to pay: This ride requires an admission pass. A three-day ticket costs $4.00 per carload.

Park officials are experimenting with planting grasses to filter runoff pollution that now seeps into the creeks. They hope that these watercourses will supply potable water in just a few years. If so, hot cyclists will probably be among the first to dunk their heads and drink deeply.

LOCAL INFORMATION

◆ Prince William County–Greater Manassas Chamber of Commerce, 8963 Center Street, Manassas, VA 20110; (703) 368–6600.
◆ Prince William Forest National Park, (703) 221–4706

LOCAL EVENTS/ATTRACTIONS

◆ Please call the Prince William Forest Park office (above) for events at the time of your visit.

ACCOMMODATIONS

♦ Alexandria Hotel Association Accommodation, (800) 296–1000. This organization will check availability and rates, and make reservations at hotels.

BIKE SHOPS

♦ Big Wheel Bikes, 2 Prince Street, Alexandria, VA 22314; (703) 739–2300.

MAPS

♦ *Arlington, Virginia, Bikeway Map and Guide.* Published by the Arlington County Department of Public Works. Free. Contact Public Works Planning Division, No. 1 Court House Plaza, 2100 North Clarendon Boulevard, Arlington, VA 22201; (703) 228–3681.

♦ *Virginia Atlas and Gazetteer.* Published by DeLorme Mapping Company. Includes topographic maps, hike/bike trails, canoeing areas. $12.95. Available at bookstores.

♦ *ADC's Washington Area Bike Map.* Compiled by Metropolitan Washington Council of Governments. $10.95. Available at bookstores and newsstands.

♦ *D.C. Bikeways.* Series of maps published by the city. $3.00. Write to District of Columbia Office of Documents, 441 Fourth Street N.W., Suite 520, Washington, D.C. 20001; (202) 727–5090.

Prince George's
Urban Farmland Ramble

J ust like Prince William Forest Park, the Beltsville Agricultural Research Center provides an oasis of green in a rapidly urbanizing area. Whereas the park offers a pristine look at acres of woodlands, the research center preserves another vanishing landscape: that of the American farm.

As the center says in its own brochure, "From the air, the center looks like a 9-mile-long, 4-mile-wide quilted blanket of green fields, pastures, and orchards." All this can be found only 15 miles northeast of the city. Along with the quiet roads, this makes the center a favorite both for bike racers in training and day-trippers coming from the neighboring University of Maryland.

Located on 7,500 acres in Prince George's County, Maryland, the center was created in 1910 to study better means of soil conservation and animal husbandry. Its nucleus was a 475-acre farm acquired by the federal government at that time. Among the notable results of research conducted here are the plump-breasted Thanksgiving turkey (the one the Pilgrims ate was a stringy wild turkey), the "modern hog" (it's leaner and longer than the old-fashioned pig and has an extra vertebra for more chops), the Atlantic potato (good for low-fat chips), and the domestic strawberry. Today the research center is devoted primarily to studies of the environment and global food supplies. It is operated by the U.S. Department of Agriculture, which maintains on the grounds more than 1,000 buildings and thousands of cattle, turkeys, and chickens.

Start: Parking lot at the NASA visitor center

Distance: 15-mile loop

Approximate pedaling time: 90 minutes

Terrain and surface: Rolling; country roads, wide shoulder

Things to see: Rustic farm buildings, fields, ponds, log cabin, and creeks

Traffic and hazards: Traffic is light early in the morning

Facilities: Rest rooms at Goddard Space Flight Center and Agriculture Research Visitor's Center (weekdays)

Option: Visit Goddard Space Flight Center

Getting there: From Washington Beltway (I-495) drive to Greenbelt exit (Route 193). Take 193 to Soil Conservation Service Road and turn left. In 100 yards, turn left at light onto Explorer Road. Park at NASA visitor center on left.

Many of those buildings are of the rustic variety: great wooden silos, rambling, weathered barns, and clapboard farmhouses with sagging front porches. What it amounts to (for the cyclist, at least) is a wide-open space in a region where that's rare. The roads are well paved. Some have broad, clean shoulders, while others are somewhat narrow.

Particularly when traffic is light early in the morning, the ride is a delight. The loop described in this ride is only a sample—there are other quiet lanes to explore as well. You'll pass ponds, stands of hardwood, pastures full of cows and sheep, a strawberry patch, orchards, old railroad tracks, and two creeks.

The center once looked inward and did not encourage public visitation, but it now encourages both recreation and education. In 1989 the center dedicated a new visitor center in a restored log cabin, originally modeled after the lodges in Yellowstone National Park. The so-called Log Lodge was built from 1934 to 1937 by the Civilian Conservation Corps (CCC) from timbers 40 to 50 feet long, harvested and milled on site. The CCC also built the major roads through the facility. Until 1985 the lodge was used as a cafeteria, where diners included Dwight D. Eisenhower and Nikita Khrushchev. It stands on Powder Mill Road on the western portion of this route. The restoration cost more than $500,000. Go in to get a map and see the exhibits.

On the way in or out, you can visit the visitor center at the Goddard Space Flight Center, a NASA research facility with a $1 billion annual budget and 12,000 employees. The museum at the center offers film clips in an eight-screen cinema, a solar telescope for sunspot viewing, an outdoor rocket park, and a simulated space-flight trainer. It's open daily from 9:00 A.M. to 4:00 P.M. One-hour-long tours are available every day. The center also hosts model-rocket launches two Sunday afternoons a month. Admission is free. Call (301) 286–8981 for more information.

Log Lodge—Visitor Center

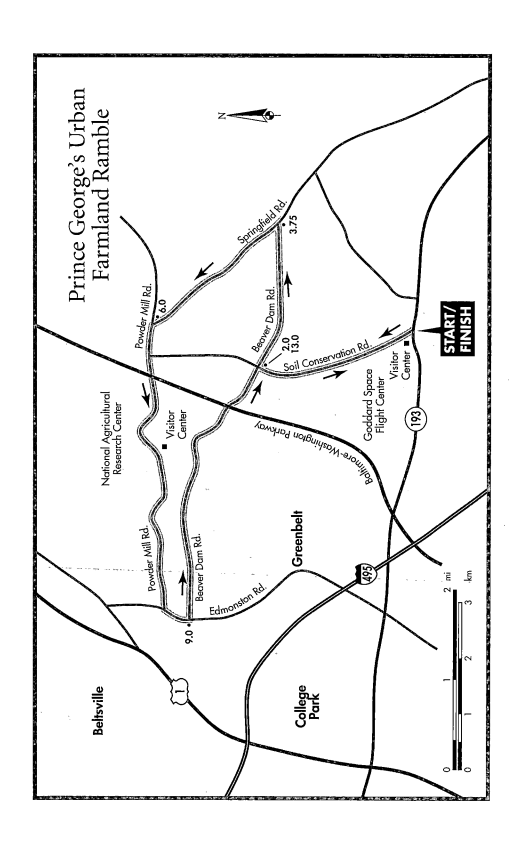

0.0 From parking lot at NASA visitor center, ride back to traffic light at Soil Conservation Road (SCS Road), and turn left.

2.0 Head north on SCS Road to Beaver Dam Road; turn right.

3.75 Sharp left onto Springfield Road.

6.0 Left onto Powder Mill Road. Pass turnoff for Soil Conservation Road on left. Look for driveway to log cabin visitor center on left.

9.0 Left onto Edmonston Road.

9.2 In about 0.2 mile, left onto Beaver Dam Road.

13.0 Right onto SCS Road to return to start.

LOCAL INFORMATION

♦ Conference and Visitors Bureau of Montgomery County, Maryland, Inc., 11820 Parklawn Drive, Suite 380, Rockville, MD 20852; (301) 428–9702 or (800) 925–0880.

♦ Montgomery County Recreation Department, 12210 Bushey Drive, Silver Spring, MD 20902; (240) 777–6804 (general information—recording).

♦ Prince George's Chamber of Commerce, 4640 Forbes Boulevard, Suite 130, Lanham, MD 20706; (301) 731–5000.

LOCAL EVENTS/ATTRACTIONS

♦ Rock Creek Park, Washington, D.C.; www.nps.gov. Luckily for Washingtonians, in 1890 Congress prevented this 1,800-acre green valley that cuts a swathe from Georgetown north through the city to the Maryland state line from becoming the unofficial city dump. Today this tranquil urban valley is a haven for bikers, joggers, and picnickers. It is a place where people can enjoy themselves, sitting quietly under the shade trees along the banks of the creek, cooking over a barbecue grill, or enjoying the sight and fragrance of the daffodils and other flowers that bloom here each spring. Visit the Rock Creek Park Nature Center at 5200 Glover Road (202–426–6828) or, for horseback riding and lessons, visit the Horse Centre off Military Road at 5100 Glover Road (202) 362–0117.

ACCOMMODATIONS

♦ Bed & Breakfast Accommodations, P.O. Box 12011, Washington, D.C. 20005; (202) 328–3510; www.bnbaccom.com.

♦ Washington D.C. Accommodations, 2201 Wisconsin Avenue, Suite C110, Washington, D.C. 20007; (202) 289–2220 or (800) 554–2220; www.wdac hotels.com.

BIKE SHOPS

♦ Revolution Cycles, at the foot of Key Bridge, 3411 M Street N.W., Washington, D.C. 20007; (202) 965–3601.
♦ The Bicycle Pro Shop, 3403 M Street, N.W., Washington, D.C. 20007; (202) 337–0311.
♦ Big Wheel Bikes, 1034 Thirty-third Street N.W., Washington, D.C. 20007; (202) 337–0254.
♦ Big Wheel Bikes, 6917 Arlington Road, Bethesda, MD 20814; (301) 652–0192.

REST ROOMS

♦ At NASA Goddard Space Flight Center and Agriculture Research Visitor's Center (weekdays).

MAPS

♦ *ADC's Washington Area Bike Map*. Compiled by Metropolitan Washington Council of Governments. $10.95. Available at bookstores and newsstands.
♦ *D.C. Bikeways*. Series of maps published by the city. $3.00. Write to District of Columbia Office of Documents, 441 Fourth Street N.W., Suite 520, Washington, D.C. 20001; (202) 727–5090.
♦ *Maryland Bicycle Touring Map*. Free. Available from Office of Tourism Development, 45 Calvert Street, Annapolis, MD 21401.
♦ *Trails in Montgomery County Parks*. Contact Maryland–National Capital Park and Planning Commission (MNCPPC), 8787 Georgia Avenue N.W., Silver Spring, MD 20910; (301) 495–2503; www.mncppc.org.

Two Creeks of Maryland Ramble

*W*hen it comes to development of off-road multiuse trails, Prince George's and eastern Montgomery Counties in Maryland are quickly catching up with their neighbors. This ride connects two off-road trails along Sligo Creek Parkway and the Northwest Branch of the Anacostia River, each traversing bucolic parks. They are particularly worth exploring if you live in the area and bicycle with a young family. The quiet, 5-mile-long Northwest Branch is a good venue to graduate youngsters from training wheels.

The ride starts at Montgomery County's Wheaton Regional Park, just 6 miles north of Washington. Look around a bit before you leave. On 496 acres, the park includes a hockey-size, open-air ice rink (I've even cycled to my skating sessions in winter), Brookside Gardens (second only to the National Arboretum in its seasonal floral display), a miniature railway with a brand-new station house, and a merry-go-round.

The off-road trail heads south through quiet suburban neighborhoods and along Sligo Creek Park, which is roughly akin to Rock Creek Park for this area of Maryland. The trail parallels the Sligo Creek Parkway, a two-lane road that winds through some pretty Takoma Park neighborhoods. The motorists are used to seeing cyclists, but take extra care to be safe and visible nonetheless. If you chose to ride on the parkway, be aware that the shoulder is quite narrow, if not nonexistent.

The parkway ends at New Hampshire Avenue, and the bike path takes a temporary detour around an area where bridge repairs are needed. From here an on-road route through neighborhoods will connect you to the restored Adelphi Mill, built in 1790 by two brothers from Pennsylvania

Start: Wheaton Regional Park

Distance: 13 miles, one way

Approximate pedaling time: 3 hours

Terrain and surface: Flat; paved off-road trails with one major intersection

Things to see: Historic mill, woodlands, suburban neighborhoods

Traffic and hazards: Riggs Road is busy

Facilities: Rest rooms, playgrounds, snack bar at Wheaton Park

Options: Rock Creek Park, Mormon Temple

Getting there: By auto, take exit 21 from the Beltway (Route 495) to Georgia Avenue (Route 97). Turn right onto Arcola Avenue and left onto Kemp Mill Road to park entrance.

(hence "Adelphi"), abandoned in 1850, and restored (albeit not to working condition) in the 1950s. One of the only two surviving gristmills in Prince George's County, it's used today for weddings and meetings.

The mill is located midway through a 5-mile stretch of off-road trail parallel to the Northwest Branch. This tributary of the Anacostia River is well stocked with trout by the U.S. Fish and Wildlife Service. Located just steps away is the miller's cottage, built of fieldstone in 1792 and now leased as a private residence for the county archaeologist.

The ravine is deep and wild looking, but the path is flat and quiet. There are some mica-covered boulders in the stream, a duck pond, and a portion of streambed full of submerged carbonized logs. These soggy hunks of driftwood are estimated to be more than 120 million years old. If removed from their aquatic state, they would disintegrate.

Like Sligo Creek, this oblong park straddles Prince George's and Montgomery Counties.

LOCAL INFORMATION

♦ D.C. Chamber of Commerce, 1213 K Street N.W., Washington, D.C. 20005; (202) 347–7201.

♦ Conference and Visitors Bureau of Montgomery County, MD, Inc., 11820 Parklawn Drive, Suite 380, Rockville, MD 20852; (301) 428–9702 or (800) 925–0880.

♦ Montgomery County Recreation Department, 12210 Bushey Drive, Silver Spring, MD 20902; (240) 777–6804 (general information—recording).

LOCAL EVENTS/ATTRACTIONS

♦ Rock Creek Park, Washington, D.C.; www.nps.gov. Luckily for Washingtonians, in 1890 Congress prevented this 1,800-acre green valley that cuts a swathe from Georgetown north through the city to the Maryland state line from becoming the unofficial city dump. Today this tranquil urban valley is a haven for bikers, joggers, and picnickers. It is a place where people can enjoy themselves, sitting quietly under the shade trees along the banks of the creek, cooking over a barbecue grill, or enjoying the sight and fragrance of the daffodils and other flowers that bloom here each spring.

◆ Rock Creek Park Nature Center & Planetarium, 5200 Glover Road N.W., Washington, D.C.; (202) 426–6829. A spot where you can see live and mounted wildlife displays, environmental exhibits, and planetarium shows, as well as participate in guided nature walks. For horseback-riding lessons, visit the Horse Centre off Military Road at 5100 Glover Road N.W. Call (202) 362–0117.

ACCOMMODATIONS

◆ Bed & Breakfast Accommodations, P.O. Box 12011, Washington, D.C. 20005; (202) 328–3510; www.bnbaccom.com.

◆ Washington D.C. Accommodations, 2201 Wisconsin Avenue, Suite C110, Washington, D.C. 20007; (202) 289–2220 or (800) 554–2220; www.wdcahotels. com.

◆ Bethesda Marriott Hotel, 5151 Pooks Hill Road, Bethesda, MD 20814; (301) 897–9400 or (800) 228–9290; fax (301) 897–4156.

◆ Holiday Inn Select Bethesda, 8120 Wisconsin Avenue, Bethesda, MD 20814; (301) 652–2000 or (800) HOLIDAY; fax (301) 652–4525.

BIKE SHOPS

◆ Revolution Cycles, at the foot of Key Bridge, 3411 M Street N.W., Washington, D.C. 20007; (202) 965–3601.

◆ The Bicycle Pro Shop, 3403 M Street, N.W., Washington, D.C. 20007; (202) 337–0311.

◆ Big Wheel Bikes, 1034 Thirty-third Street N.W., Washington, D.C.; (202) 337–0254.

◆ Big Wheel Bikes, 6917 Arlington Road, Bethesda, MD 20814; (301) 652–0192.

MAPS

◆ *ADC's Washington Area Bike Map*. Compiled by Metropolitan Washington Council of Governments. $10.95. Available at bookstores and newsstands.

◆ *D.C. Bikeways*. Series of maps published by the city. $3.00. Write to District of Columbia Office of Documents, 441 Fourth Street N.W., Suite 520, Washington, D.C. 20001; (202) 727–5090.

◆ *Maryland Bicycle Touring Map*. Free. Available from Office of Tourism Development, 45 Calvert Street, Annapolis, MD 21401.

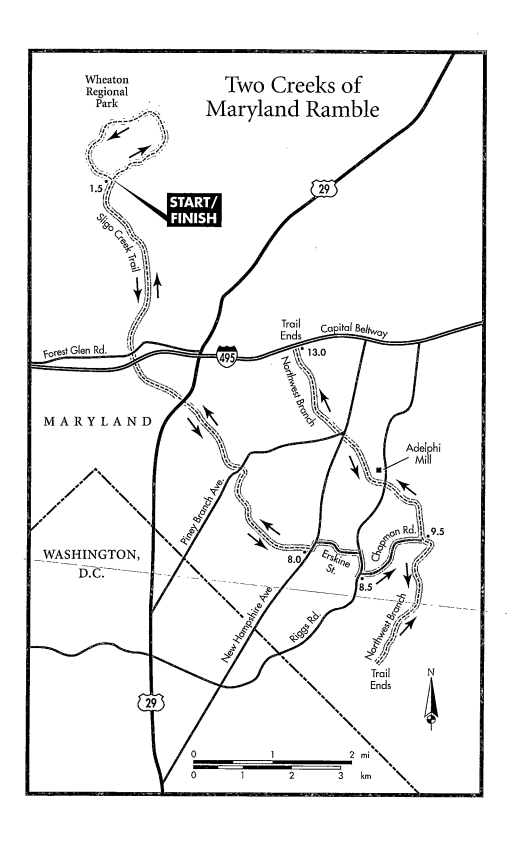

Two Creeks of Maryland Ramble

Wheaton
Regional
Park

START/
FINISH

1.5

Sligo Creek Trail

29

Forest Glen Rd.

495

Trail
Ends

Capital Beltway

13.0

Northwest Branch

MARYLAND

Adelphi
Mill

Piney Branch Ave.

Chapman Rd.

9.5

WASHINGTON,
D.C.

8.0

Erskine
St.

8.5

New Hampshire Ave.

Riggs Rd.

Northwest Branch

Trail
Ends

N

29

| 0 | | 1 | | 2 | mi |
| 0 | 1 | 2 | | 3 | km |

0.0 Start at Wheaton Regional Park, Orebaugh and Arcola Avenues, Wheaton, Maryland. Ride loop road around park.

1.5 Ride south on Sligo Creek hiker/biker trail (off-road).

8.0 Sligo Creek Parkway ends at New Hampshire Avenue. Turn left onto New Hampshire and immediately right onto Erskine Street.

8.5 Right onto Riggs Road (busy).

9.0 Left onto Chapman Road.

9.5 Right onto Northwest Branch hiker/biker trail (off-road).

At end of park, turn around and double back. Cross Riggs Road to reach historic Adelphi Mill and continue to northern end of park.

Option: Connection to Rock Creek Park (2 miles).
♦ Head south from Wheaton Regional Park, as stated above.
♦ Just before passing under Beltway Bridge, turn right onto Forest Glen Road.
♦ At intersection of Seminary Road, turn right onto Capitol View Avenue.
♦ Capitol View becomes Stoneybrook, which ends at Beach Drive (Rock Creek Park).

Option: While on Stonybrook, turn right into visitor center for Mormon Temple (see Ride 4).

♦ *Trails in Montgomery County Parks.* Contact Maryland–National Capital Park and Planning Commission (MNCPPC), 8787 Georgia Avenue N.W., Silver Spring, MD 20910; (301) 495–2503; www.mncppc.org.

Around Avenel Ramble

A PIECE OF POTOMAC

F ar from my tie-dyed, gritty town of Takoma Park ("where old hippies go to die") lies a land of horse farms and houses the size of small hotels, five-car garages, and home squash courts. It's Potomac, Maryland, the Washington area's own East Egg, and it's threaded with some two-lane blacktop that beckons cyclists. This chapter outlines a figure eight that's a great training ride.

A bit of background. Until 1880, Potomac was called Offutt's Crossroads, named for the area's largest landowners. It remained sleepy and rural until the early part of the century, when some fields were turned into estates. Additional cachet came with the 1924 opening of the Congressional Country Club, followed by the 1930 founding of the Potomac Hunt Club: A squirearchy was born. Potomac residents today are more likely to go golfing or shopping than foxhunting, but the area has retained many horse pastures and bridle paths. Equestrian fever still runs high.

Start at Avenel, a 1,000-acre former horse farm that's now a luxury housing development centered on a new 225-acre, professional-circuit golf course. Avenel is packed with visual niceties and amenities: meadows, rows of freshly planted trees, iron lampposts, preserved forests. Even the brass-plated, neo-everything architecture isn't bad by local standards.

Begin in the gravel parking area of the equestrian center, where pastures engulf a fine old timber-frame horse barn. After heading down a short drive, take a right if you want to see the Tournament Players Club, where as many as 32,000 people convene each May to watch the Kemper Open golf tournament.

Otherwise, turn left onto Clubhouse Road to start the ride.

A right onto Oaklyn Drive takes you past the information center (they were nice to me despite my gritty bike clothes), where you can get the scoop on million-dollar homes in eight separate Avenel developments. The pool-table-smooth road provides entertaining dips and turns, and the scenery is impeccably groomed. Even the meadows of goldenrod and second-growth forests look picked over and arranged. The housing cluster on the right is called Player's Crossing; on the left is Player's Gate. (The developer calls these villages, but if they are, I'm Greg LeMond.)

Turn left onto Persimmon Tree Road and leave Avenel for an older neighborhood of grand ranch houses and Tudors mixed in with new "tract mansions," as Henry Allen of the *Washington Post* dubs Potomac's large new houses. The road surface remains superb. Persimmon Tree winds a bit until you come to a busy, oblique intersection with River Road. Be careful of heavy traffic here. Turn right to stay on this route; turn left if you need refreshments in the Potomac Village shopping area, less than 0.3 mile down River Road. There's a trendy patisserie and gourmet coffee shop as well as a grocery store.

Back on the route, follow River Road east for about 1.5 miles. This is a busy, two-lane arterial, but there's a parallel path for bailing out if you feel uncomfortable in traffic. It's a straight shot past more big homes until you turn right at a traffic light onto Bradley Boulevard.

Bradley is more lightly traveled, but there is also an adjacent path available, smooth, albeit narrow. Proceed to a four-way stop at the intersection with Persimmon Tree. Take a left (this is the knot in the figure eight) to explore a new part of Persimmon Tree. You pass another part of Avenel ("Willowgate"), cross the Capital Beltway on an overpass, and descend to the bluffs of the Potomac River. At this midpoint of the ride, if you are in need of refreshment, you can turn left onto MacArthur Boulevard to a shopping center with a natural food store and deli. Now heading west on MacArthur Boulevard, you're rid-

THE BASICS

Start: Equestrian center

Distance: 14 miles

Approximate pedaling time: 90 minutes

Terrain and surface: Rolling; smooth roads, some with adjacent off-road trails

Things to see: Stream-cut ravines, meadows, ritzy neighborhoods

Traffic and hazards: The Persimmon Tree and River Road intersection is very busy

Facilities: PGA golf course, Potomac Village and MacArthur Plaza shopping areas with food, banks, rest rooms

Option: Visit Great Falls Tavern and Visitor's Center

Getting there: By car, take Route 495 to River Road West (exit 39). Turn left on Bradley Boulevard. At four-way stop, go straight to pick up Oaklyn Drive. Turn left onto Clubhouse Road. Take first right into equestrian center.

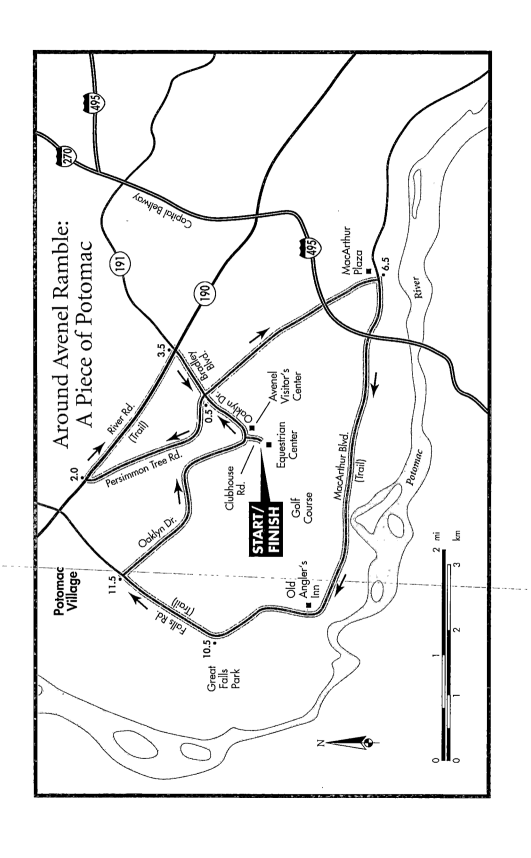

Around Avenel Ramble: A Piece of Potomac

0.0 Leave equestrian center via driveway and left onto Clubhouse Road.
0.1 At T intersection, right onto Oaklyn Drive.
0.5 At four-way stop, left onto Persimmon Tree Road.
2.0 At oblique T intersection, right onto River Road (Route 190). Take bike path on left.
3.5 At four-way intersection with traffic light, right onto Bradley Boulevard (Route 191).
4.0 At four-way stop, left onto Persimmon Tree Road.
6.5 At T intersection at bottom of hill, right onto MacArthur Boulevard.
        Option: Ride left on MacArthur Boulevard for 0.4 mile to shops/rest rooms.
10.5 Right onto Falls Road.
11.5 Right onto Oaklyn Drive.
13.5 Right onto Clubhouse Road.
13.6 Right into equestrian center.

ing through a neighborhood mixing older bungalows with newer homes and dense vegetation. On the left you'll pass the Naval Surface Warfare Center, which is a research facility, not a dock or shipyard. What looks like a mile-long Quonset hut is used for testing scale-model ships. Just over the horizon find the Carderock Recreation Area (a mecca for rock climbers and rappellers), rapids of the Potomac, and islands named Offutt, Turkey, Vaso, Hermit, and Perry.

MacArthur Boulevard is popular for serious cyclists in training. To its credit, Montgomery County has alerted drivers with recently posted SHARE THE ROAD signs. There's also an adjacent off-road trail/shoulder. I'd rather ride the road; stick to the shoulder if you prefer a 10-mph pace, cars bother you, or you're riding with children.

At Old Angler's Inn, follow the road to the right as it begins a mile-long climb through dense woods. There's a nice, wide shoulder along this stretch. The next turn is a right onto Falls Road. You have the option of turning left and descending into Great Falls Park, where you can just explore a while and return to your route, or pick up the C & O Canal Trail and ride a dozen miles back to Washington. If you're staying with the route, be alert, as Falls Road is narrow and crowded. Again, an adjacent trail on the left offers a way out. A right turn onto Oaklyn Drive brings you through more of Avenel ("Oaklyn Woods," "Chartwell") through open space set aside for the future water-treatment plant. Just before the open space, look closely for the village of Pleasant Gate. You'll immediately sense this section is quite different from its surroundings. The homes are only one story and attached. These sixty homes were built to pro-

Potomac River

vide "moderate income housing," and twenty are still held by the county housing authority for low-income tenants. You can bet the waiting list is long! Stay on Oaklyn until Clubhouse Road, where you can return to the equestrian center's parking area.

LOCAL INFORMATION

♦ D.C. Chamber of Commerce, 1213 K Street N.W., Washington, D.C. 20005; (202) 347–7201.
♦ Conference and Visitors Bureau of Montgomery County, MD, Inc., 11820 Parklawn Drive, Suite 380, Rockville, MD 20852; (301) 428–9702 or (800) 925–0880.
♦ Montgomery County Recreation Department, 12210 Bushey Drive, Silver Spring, MD 20902; (240) 777–6804 (general information—recording).

LOCAL EVENTS/ATTRACTIONS

♦ Historic Glen Echo buildings along the route.
♦ Clara Barton National Historic Site.

ACCOMMODATIONS

♦ Old Angler's Inn, 10801 MacArthur Boulevard, Potomac, MD 20854; (301) 299–9097.
♦ Bed & Breakfast Accommodations, P.O. Box 12011, Washington, D.C. 20005; (202) 328–3510; www.bnbaccom.com.
♦ Washington D.C. Accommodations, 2201 Wisconsin Avenue, Suite C110, Washington, D.C. 20007; (202) 289–2220 or (800) 554–2220; www.wdcahotels. com.

BIKE SHOPS

♦ Revolution Cycles, at the foot of Key Bridge, 3411 M Street N.W., Washington, D.C. 20007; (202) 965–3601.
♦ The Bicycle Pro Shop, 3403 M Street N.W., Washington, DC 20007; (202) 337–0311.
♦ Big Wheel Bikes, 1034 Thirty-third Street NW, Washington, D.C. 20007; (202) 337–0254.

MAPS

♦ ADC's *Washington Area Bike Map.* Compiled by Metropolitan Washington Council of Governments. $10.95. Available at bookstores and newsstands.

◆ *D.C. Bikeways.* Series of maps published by the city. $3.00. Write to District of Columbia Office of Documents, 441 Fourth Street NW, Suite 520, Washington, D.C. 20001; (202) 727–5090.

◆ *Maryland Bicycle Touring Map.* Free. Available from Office of Tourism Development, 45 Calvert Street, Annapolis, MD 21401.

◆ *Trails in Montgomery County Parks.* Contact Maryland–National Capital Park and Planning Commission (MNCPPC), 8787 Georgia Avenue N.W., Silver Spring, MD 20910; (301) 495–2503; www.mncppc.org.

Edwards Ferry Cruise

This loop explores the Potomac's scenic bottomlands, where a slower, straighter part of the river above Great Falls glides by cornfields, swamps, sod farms, oak forest, and ruins. It's a good ride to append to Ride 24 (Sugarland Loop Ramble) or Ride 25 (Escape to the Maryland Countryside Challenge), but it also stands well on its own.

Start about 15 miles west of D.C. at the Sycamore Landing parking area of the C & O Canal. This is the land of Seneca sandstone, the building material for the Smithsonian Castle and other Washington landmarks. Sycamore Landing is an old canal landing abandoned in 1924 with the rest of the C & O. The canal is dry here, and a hardwood forest is overtaking its bed. You can look over the Potomac to Maddox Island.

Ride away from the canal through McKee-Beshers Wildlife Area, which looks like a farm because its lowland fields are sown with corn and other plants that attract wildlife. The wildlife attract hunters, so expect gunfire in hunting season. Cross Horsepen Branch on a bridge and turn left onto River Road, which becomes Old River Road when it narrows suddenly to one lane and enters the woods. (This was an Indian path later used to roll hogsheads of tobacco to Georgetown.) There's a grade to climb here with a view of a hardwood swamp on the left. I've seen red-tailed hawks perched on the snags of dead sycamores. Be looking for bits of prickly pear clinging to rock outcrops on the right. The cactus is native to the East.

Past a shale rock face, pass through a mile-long lawn—a sod farm. The scenery becomes vaguely British when hedgerows appear, but less so where large homes on five-acre lots have replaced eroded farmland. Several large horse farms and Montgomery County's enlightened rural preservation program have helped save a semblance of countryside. Glide down Edwards Ferry

THE BASICS

Start: Sycamore Landing parking areas

Distance: 21-mile loop

Approximate pedaling time: 2 hours

Terrain and surface: Mostly flat, some hills; smooth two-lane roads and dirt towpath

Things to see: Ruins at Edwards Ferry, farm country, wildlife area, swamp, C & O Canal, one-room schoolhouse

Traffic and hazards: Light traffic

Facilities: Camping, stores, and rest rooms at Riley's Lock and pit, en route

Getting there: Take Beltway to River Road West (exit 39). Follow River Road through Potomac Village. Bear left at sign for Route 112 to stay on River Road. After passing Hughes Road on right, take next left onto Sycamore Landing Road (unpaved) and park at end, next to C & O Canal.

Road past fields once strewn with cobblestones and boulders (this was the prehistoric Potomac's bed when the river was much higher). There are still some rocks in these Piedmont fields.

At Edwards Ferry there's a well-preserved lock house and the stone-and-brick ruins of a grain warehouse. The ferry landing was once a transfer point for wagonloads of grain, coal, and supplies. Across this wide, fairly calm part of the Potomac is Virginia's Goose Creek. Unfortunately, this natural area now sports a golf course.

Pick up the towpath for a return past Sycamore Landing and on to another well-maintained lock named Riley's. The towpath can get pretty muddy along this stretch, but it's not so bad that you would need a mountain bike. There's camping on the canal at Chisel Branch Hiker-Biker Camp (water pumps and outhouse available), but check ahead to see if you need reservations (202–653–5190).

After visiting Riley's Lock, described in Ride 24, follow Riley's Lock Road to River Road, and turn left at Poole's Country Store. Shortly, you'll pass the Seneca Schoolhouse Museum. This one-room schoolhouse was constructed in 1886 of the same locally quarried sandstone used to build the Smithsonian Castle. The school was used until 1910, then converted to a private residence until 1981 when the building was restored to its original state. The original wood floors are intact, and some of the original desks remain.

The schoolhouse is open every Sunday from March to December. By appointment, the school is operated as a living classroom, with costumed docents providing a full day of 1880s-style schooling for field trips.

Complete your ride down River Road and back into Sycamore Landing. On my most recent ride, I was pleasantly surprised to see a flock of wild turkeys at this point.

LOCAL INFORMATION

♦ D.C. Chamber of Commerce, 1213 K Street N.W., Washington, D.C. 20005; (202) 347–7201.

Riley's Lock

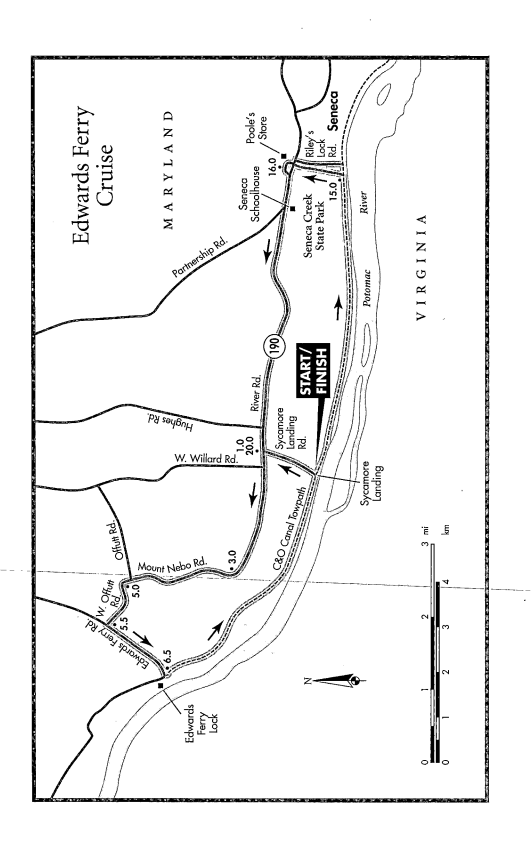

Edwards Ferry
Cruise

M A R Y L A N D

Partnership Rd.

Seneca
Schoolhouse

Poole's
Store

Seneca

Riley's
Lock
Rd.

16.0

Seneca Creek
State Park

15.0

Hughes Rd.

River Rd.

190

START/
FINISH

W. Willard Rd.

1.0
20.0

Sycamore
Landing
Rd.

Sycamore
Landing

Potomac
River

VIRGINIA

Offutt Rd.

Mount Nebo Rd.

3.0

C&O Canal Towpath

W. Offutt Rd.

5.0

Edwards Ferry Rd.

5.5

6.5

Edwards
Ferry
Lock

N

0   1   2   3 mi

0   1   2   3   4 km

0.0	North (away from canal) on Sycamore Landing Road (unpaved).
1.0	Left onto River Road.
3.0	Bear right on Mount Nebo Road.
5.0	Left onto West Offutt Road.
5.5	Left onto Edwards Ferry Road.
6.5	Left onto towpath. Pass Sycamore Landing.
15.0	Left onto Riley's Lock Road.
16.0	Left onto River Road (store across street).
20.0	Left onto Sycamore Landing Road.

♦ Conference and Visitors Bureau of Montgomery County, Maryland, Inc., 11820 Parklawn Drive, Suite 380, Rockville, MD 20852; (301) 428–9702 or (800) 925–0880.
♦ Montgomery County Recreation Department, 12210 Bushey Drive, Silver Spring, MD 20902; (240) 777–6804 (general information—recording).

LOCAL EVENTS/ATTRACTIONS

♦ Riley's Lock along the route.

ACCOMMODATIONS

♦ Old Angler's Inn, 10801 MacArthur Boulevard, Potomac, MD 20854; (301) 299–9097.
♦ Bed & Breakfast Accommodations, P.O. Box 12011, Washington, DC 20005; (202) 328–3510; www.bnbaccom.com.
♦ Washington D.C. Accommodations, 2201 Wisconsin Avenue, Suite C110, Washington, D.C. 20007; (202) 289–2220 or (800) 554–2220; www.wdcahotels. com.

BIKE SHOPS

♦ Revolution Cycles, at the foot of Key Bridge, 3411 M Street N.W., Washington, D.C. 20007; (202) 965–3601.
♦ The Bicycle Pro Shop, 3403 M Street, N.W., Washington, D.C. 20007; (202) 337–0311.
♦ Big Wheel Bikes, 1034 Thirty-third Street N.W., Washington, D.C. 20007; (202) 337–0254.

MAPS

♦ *ADC's Washington Area Bike Map.* Compiled by Metropolitan Washington Council of Governments. $10.95. Available at bookstores and newsstands.

♦ *D.C. Bikeways.* Series of maps published by the city. $3.00. Write to District of Columbia Office of Documents, 441 Fourth Street N.W., Suite 520, Washington, D.C. 20001; (202) 727–5090.

♦ *Maryland Bicycle Touring Map.* Free. Available from Office of Tourism Development, 45 Calvert Street, Annapolis, MD 21401.

♦ *Trails in Montgomery County Parks.* Contact Maryland–National Capital Park and Planning Commission (MNCPPC), 8787 Georgia Avenue N.W., Silver Spring, MD 20910; (301) 495–2503; www.mncppc.org.

Sugarland Loop Ramble

H ere's one of the sweetest rides in Montgomery Country—a little corner of road-cycling heaven within forty-five minutes of downtown Washington. The Sugarland Loop lies in the county's northwest corner, long a favorite destination for area cyclists. You'll be likely to run into group rides organized by the Potomac Pedalers Club or training rides organized by any of the several local racing clubs.

The Sugarland Loop is a perfect 13-mile jaunt. For a longer ride, combine it with Ride 23 (Edwards Ferry Cruise). For a *really* long ride, try Ride 25 (Escape to the Maryland Countryside Challenge), which covers some of the same roads.

Start at Riley's Lock, off River Road just west of Seneca Road. The parking lot here provides a convenient staging area not only for cyclists but also for hikers heading out on the C & O Canal towpath, for picnickers using the grassy park on the river, and for boaters putting in at Seneca Creek for easy access to the Potomac. Be sure to take a look at the aqueduct, which used to carry the canal *over* Seneca Creek on its way west. Its huge blocks of Seneca sandstone still arch over the wide creek, but the canal dried up along here years ago.

Ride back toward River Road along Riley's Lock Road, which provides a nice creekside warm-up. Then turn west onto River Road, shortly passing by the Seneca Schoolhouse Museum, described in Ride 23. Keep an eye out for your right turn onto Partnership Road.

Partnership Road is a cyclist's dream road—few cars, lined by woods and horse farms, a polo club, very few houses and driveways, just one intersection, just a couple of hills. Nothing could be simpler or nicer.

Then make a sharp right onto White's Ferry Road. This is also a beautiful stretch of roadway, but more heavily traveled.

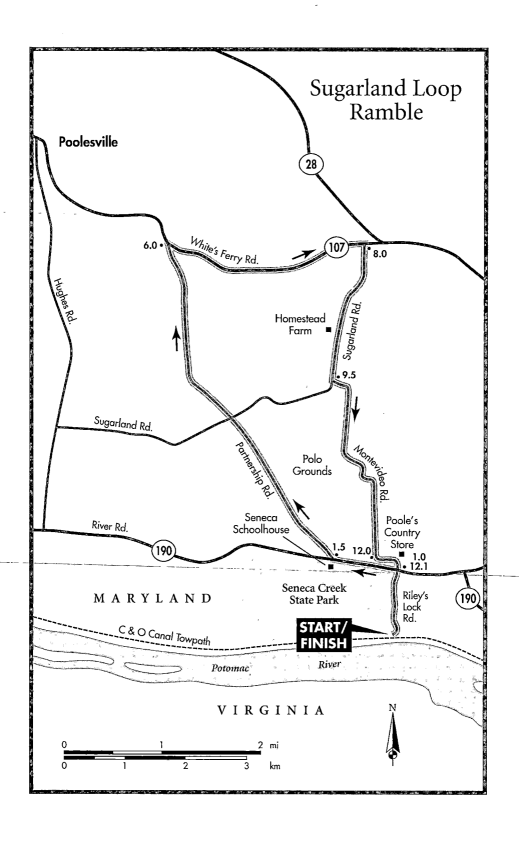

Sugarland Loop Ramble

Poolesville

28

6.0 · White's Ferry Rd. → 107 · 8.0

Hughes Rd.

Homestead Farm ■

Sugarland Rd.

· 9.5

Sugarland Rd.

Partnership Rd.

Polo Grounds

Montevideo Rd.

River Rd.

Seneca Schoolhouse

Poole's Country Store
■ 1.0
· 12.1

190

1.5 12.0 ·

MARYLAND

Seneca Creek State Park

Riley's Lock Rd.

190

START/ FINISH

C & O Canal Towpath

Potomac   River

VIRGINIA   N

0 ——————— 1 ——————— 2 mi
0 ——— 1 ——— 2 ——— 3 km

Turn right after a few miles onto Sugarland Road. You'll soon pass by Homestead Farm, which helps keep this area's agricultural tradition alive by offering pick-your-own fruits and vegetables from late May (strawberries) through October (pumpkins). If you'd like to sample the farm's offerings, make a quick detour up the driveway. The owners operate a small stand where you can buy already picked produce. If you stop, there are picnic tables to enjoy your purchases.

Soon after Homestead Farm, turn left onto Montevideo Road. You'll dive down a short hill, cross a one-lane bridge, then climb up the other side on your way to another of this area's country institutions. Poole's Country Store, located on Old River Road toward the end of

THE BASICS

Start: Riley's Lock

Distance: 12 miles

Approximate pedaling time: 90 minutes

Terrain and surface: Rolling; well-paved country roads

Things to see: Old C & O Canal aqueduct, one-room schoolhouse, Homestead Farm (for pick-your-own fruit in season)

Traffic and hazards: Light traffic

Facilities: Rest rooms at Riley's Lock, food at Poole's Country Store

Getting there: Take Beltway to River Road, west (exit 39). Follow River Road through Potomac Village. Turn left at sign for Route 112 to stay on River Road. Then, at bottom of long hill, turn left onto Riley's Lock Road. Park in lot at end of road.

this ride, is a favorite all-purpose stop. You can refill your water bottle, buy a soda or cup of coffee, pick up a sandwich, catch up on the latest community news, or just sit on the front stoop and reflect on a perfect 12-mile ride.

MILES AND DIRECTIONS

0.0 From start/finish at Riley's Lock parking area, ride away from river on Riley's Lock Road.

1.0 Left onto River Road.

1.5 Right onto Partnership Road. Follow Partnership Road to end, crossing Sugarland Road en route.

6.0 Right onto White's Ferry Road.

8.0 Right onto Sugarland Road at cluster of small houses. Ride carefully; Sugarland narrows to a single lane of concrete slab roadway with dirt shoulders. Pass Homestead Farm, a favorite pick-your-own destination, on the right.

9.5 Left onto Montevideo Road.

12.0 Left onto Old River Road just before Montevideo Road ends at (new) River Road.

12.1 Left onto River Road at Poole's Country Store (great stopping spot for refreshments!). Immediate right onto Riley's Lock Road to return to parking area.

LOCAL INFORMATION

♦ D.C. Chamber of Commerce, 1213 K Street N.W., Washington, D.C. 20005; (202) 347–7201.

♦ Conference and Visitors Bureau of Montgomery County, Maryland, Inc., 11820 Parklawn Drive, Suite 380, Rockville, MD 20852; (301) 428–9702 or (800) 925–0880.

♦ Montgomery County Recreation Department, 12210 Bushey Drive, Silver Spring, MD 20902; (240) 777–6804 (general information—recording).

LOCAL EVENTS/ATTRACTIONS

♦ Riley's Lock in Seneca. Chesapeake & Ohio Canal Visitors Center, 11710 MacArthur Boulevard, Potomac, MD 20854; (301) 767–3714; www.nps.gov/choh.

ACCOMMODATIONS

♦ Old Angler's Inn, 10801 MacArthur Boulevard, Potomac, MD 20854; (301) 299–9097.

♦ Bed & Breakfast Accommodations, P.O. Box 12011, Washington, D.C. 20005; (202) 328–3510; www.bnbaccom.com.

♦ Washington D.C. Accommodations, 2201 Wisconsin Avenue, Suite C110, Washington, D.C. 20007; (202) 289–2220 or (800) 554–2220; www.wdcahotels. com.

BIKE SHOPS

♦ Revolution Cycles, at the foot of Key Bridge, 3411 M Street N.W., Washington, D.C. 20007; (202) 965–3601.

♦ The Bicycle Pro Shop, 3403 M Street, N.W., Washington, D.C. 20007; (202) 337–0311.

♦ Big Wheel Bikes, 1034 Thirty-third Street N.W., Washington, D.C. 20007; (202) 337–0254.

MAPS

♦ *ADC's Washington Area Bike Map*. Compiled by Metropolitan Washington Council of Governments. $10.95. Available at bookstores and newsstands.

♦ *D.C. Bikeways*. Series of maps published by the city. $3.00. Write to District of Columbia Office of Documents, 441 Fourth Street N.W., Suite 520, Washington, D.C. 20001; (202) 727–5090.

♦ *Maryland Bicycle Touring Map*. Free. Available from Office of Tourism Development, 45 Calvert Street, Annapolis, MD 21401.

♦ *Trails in Montgomery County Parks*. Contact Maryland–National Capital Park and Planning Commission (MNCPPC), 8787 Georgia Avenue N.W., Silver Spring, MD 20910; (301) 495–2503; www.mncppc.org.

Escape to the Maryland
Countryside Challenge

his is a route suggested by a person who knows more about biking than almost anyone around the Beltway: Mike Dornfield, a
former associate bicycling coordinator for Washington, D.C.

Mike developed the route as a weekend getaway, but I've adapted it
as a ride from Metrorail's Red Line through the inner suburbs of
Montgomery County, with a destination of the quiet country town of
Poolesville, a Civil War site of minor importance. On the way out and
the way back you bisect the toney community of Potomac, Maryland,
where the huge houses are likely to be augmented by a horse barn and a
steeplechase course. The ride concludes with a historic section of the
Potomac River before ending in Georgetown. The optional return will
lead you back to the Metro if you parked there.

Start at Metrorail's Grosvenor Station. (This commencement point may
also be reached by riding through Rock Creek Park, as described in Rides 3 and
4.) The immediate area is strictly suburban blah, with a six-lane road and
ramps dominating the scenery. But a nifty suburban road called Tuckerman
Lane will soon whisk you away from all that. Although not designated a bike
route, Tuckerman easily accommodates two-wheelers. After starting off with
four surprisingly quiet lanes going through an area of condominium apartments, it narrows to two lanes but with a shoulder wide enough for a fire truck.

The scenery is split levels and driveways as far as the eye can see, but traffic

Horse farm in historic Poolesville

remains fairly light, and many of the yards are planted with azaleas and flowering trees. Soon you bisect the creek ravine that contains Cabin John Regional Park, which includes a petting zoo, a 1-mile minature railroad, and seven primitive campsites. At Falls Road, just past a nursery, you run into a row of small farmsteads with graceful old houses and barns, but don't be fooled—you're not in the country yet. Falls Road winds through the countrified estates of upper Potomac, where the squirearchy have maintained a semblance of the farmscape for horse pastures.

THE BASICS

Start: Grosvenor Metrorail station

Distance: 57- or 75-mile loop

Approximate pedaling time: 3 or 5 hours

Terrain and surface: Very hilly; suburban and country roads

Things to see: Horse farms, fields, historic Poolesville, Maryland, Sugarloaf Mountain; Potomac riverfront

Options: 18-mile round-trip ride to Sugarloaf Mountain; end-of-ride return to Metrorail station

Facilities: Rest rooms and food at Poole's Store, Poolesville, Potomac

Traffic and hazards: Avoid River Road traffic, which is fast moving; see Return Options in Miles and Directions

Getting there: By auto, take Beltway to exit 34; take Route 355 north to Grosvenor Station. By Metro, Red Line to Grosvenor. By bike, take path through Rock Creek Regional Park in Maryland to Route 355, turn right and right again onto Tuckerman Lane (loops around Metro station to head west).

The real country kicks in just past 5,000-acre Seneca Creek State Park at the town of Seneca. From here you can traverse roads lined with wildflowers and high meadows overlooking the Potomac, then huff and puff uphill through real horse farms until reaching the town of Poolesville, which was contested during the Civil War. Founded in 1793 by the merchant John Poole, Poolesville has remained a country town despite some recent development. There's a twenty-building historic district and several antiques shops worth visiting along its tree-lined streets.

The ride downhill from Poolesville has got to be one of the greatest delights in all of cycling. It's an almost vertical descent on a winding country road with pastures and creeks and woods and dancing figures of Queen Anne's lace creeping up to its edge. On the horizon you can sense the valley floor and the surging Potomac, while the foothills of the Blue Ridge Mountains rise into Virginia on the far side. It would be a wonderful place to watch the sun set, framed by streaking clouds and golden grasses and grains, if you didn't have many more miles to ride before dark.

Back on River Road, be prepared for more pretty scenery as you pass polo grounds, a wildlife management area, and a state park. After Riley's Lock Road, River Road turns right and subjects you to some drastic hills, and increasing traffic on the way through forests and then more estates of Potomac. Pass through

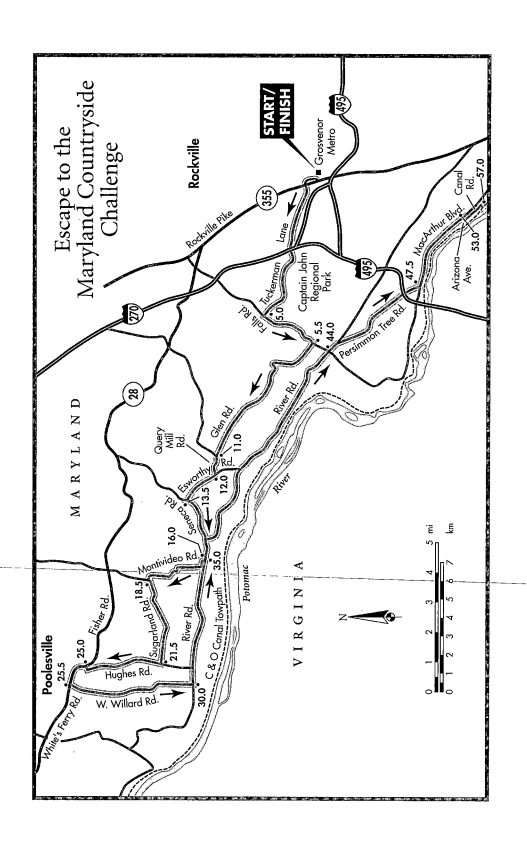

Escape to the
Maryland Countryside
Challenge

Rockville

MARYLAND

Poolesville

VIRGINIA

START/
FINISH

Grosvenor
Metro

495

270

28

355

Rockville Pike

Lane

Tuckerman

Captain John
Regional
Park

Persimmon Tree Rd.

MacArthur Blvd.

Canal
Rd.
57.0

Arizona
Ave. 53.0

47.5

5.0

5.5
44.0

Falls Rd.

Glen Rd.

11.0

Query
Mill
Rd.

Esworthy Rd.
12.0

13.5

Seneca Rd.

River Rd.

16.0

Montivideo Rd.

35.0

Fisher Rd.

18.5

Sugarland Rd.

21.5

River Rd.

25.0

Hughes Rd.

25.5

White's Ferry Rd.

W. Willard Rd.

30.0

C & O Canal Towpath

Potomac
River

N

0   1   2   3   4   5 mi

0   1   2   3   4   5   6   7 km

0.0   From Grosvenor Station, Red Line of Metrorail, take east ramp out of station to Tuckerman Lane. Turn left to head west. Cross Route 355 (traffic light) to continue on Tuckerman. Take Tuckerman past camping area and Cabin John Regional Park.

5.0   Left onto Falls Road.

5.5   First right onto Glen Road. Stay on Glen for 5.5 miles.

11.0   At T intersection, turn left, downhill, onto Query Mill Road.

12.0   After quick, brisk descent, turn right onto Esworthy Road.

13.5   At T intersection, left onto Seneca Road (Route 112). Continue straight as Seneca Road merges with River Road.

16.0   Right onto Montevideo Road (just past Poole's Country Store, a good pit stop).

18.5   At four-way intersection, left on Sugarland Road (not Sugarland Lane).

21.5   At T intersection, right onto Hughes Road. Take Hughes Road into town of Poolesville.

25.0   Left on Fisher Avenue; becomes White's Ferry Road in Poolesville.

25.5   Left onto West Willard Road (near high school).

30.0   After steep descent, left onto River Road.

35.0   Turn right with River Road as Seneca Road continues straight. (To avoid drastic hills and fast traffic on this next stretch of River Road, see Return Options.) Stay on River Road (use shoulder) through town of Potomac.

44.0   After main intersection of town of Potomac, right onto Persimmon Tree Road.

47.5   (all downhill) Left onto MacArthur Boulevard. Return to Washington via Cabin John and Glen Echo.

53.0   Back in Washington, right onto Arizona Avenue N.W.

53.25   Left onto Canal Road near railroad bridge.

53.75   Hard right at entrance to Fletcher's Boat House (canoe rental, refreshments, and fishing gear available).

57.0   Take towpath of C & O Canal to Georgetown, where ride ends.

Midride Option (18-Mile Trip to Sugarloaf Mountain):

◆ In Poolesville, left onto Fisher Avenue (Route 107).

◆ In 2 miles, right onto Wasche Road.

◆ In 2.5 miles, right onto Martinsburg Road.

◆ Left onto Dickerson Road at Darnestown Road.

◆ In Dickerson, immediate right after bridge unmarked Mount Ephraim Road; ride 2.5 miles across Barnesville Road and enter Sugarloaf preserve.

◆ Backtrack via Mount Ephraim to Barnesville Road.

◆ Left onto Barnesville Road.

◆ Right onto Peach Tree Road.

(continued)

◆ Left onto Route 28 and immediately right onto Cattail Road.
◆ Right onto Fisher Avenue in Poolesville.

Return Options: To avoid hilliest stretch of River Road, continue straight on Seneca Road at point where River Road turns right past entrance to Bretton Woods Recreation Center. Retrace route along Esworthy, Query Mill, and Glen Roads to Falls Road. Turn right onto Falls Road, then left onto River Road to continue ride to Georgetown. Or turn left onto Falls Road and pick up Tuckerman Lane back to Grosvenor Metro.

Potomac's clogged center, then turn right onto Persimmon Tree Drive to return to Washington via MacArthur Boulevard—a route described in Ride 10.

An optional return route avoids this last stretch of River Road *and* gives you the further option of returning to your starting point at the Grosvenor Metro. After passing Riley's Lock Road, simply continue straight on Seneca Road as River Road turns right. Retrace your route along Esworthy, Query Mill, Glen, Falls, and Tuckerman Roads back to the Grosvenor Station.

An optional ride from Poolesville takes you to the Washington area's only "mountain"—1,280-foot Sugarloaf Mountain, a National Historic Landmark surrounded by a 3,000-acre, privately owned preserve. Sugarloaf has been called "an outpost of the Appalachians." During the Civil War, Union troops used this precipice to observe General Robert E. Lee fording the Potomac at White's Ferry en route to Antietam Battlefield. Feeling really hardy? Ride to Sugarloaf's peak before turning back and enjoy the tremendous views.

LOCAL INFORMATION

◆ D.C. Chamber of Commerce, 1213 K Street N.W., Washington, D.C. 20005; (202) 347-7201
◆ Conference and Visitors Bureau of Montgomery County, Maryland, Inc., 11820 Parklawn Drive, Suite 380, Rockville, MD 20852; (301) 428-9702 or (800) 925-0880.
◆ Montgomery County Recreation Department, 12210 Bushey Drive, Silver Spring, MD 20902; (240) 777-6804 (general information—recording).

LOCAL EVENTS/ATTRACTIONS

◆ Cabin John Regional Park.

ACCOMMODATIONS

◆ Old Angler's Inn, 10801 MacArthur Boulevard, Potomac, MD 20854; (301) 299-9097.

◆ Bed & Breakfast Accommodations, P.O. Box 12011, Washington, D.C.; (202) 328–3510; www.bnbaccom.com.
◆ Washington D.C. Accommodations, 2201 Wisconsin Avenue, Suite C110, Washington, D.C. 20007; (202) 289–2220 or (800) 554–2220; www.wdcahotels. com.

BIKE SHOPS

◆ Revolution Cycles, at the foot of Key Bridge, 3411 M Street N.W., Washington, DC 20007; (202) 965–3601.
◆ The Bicycle Pro Shop, 3403 M Street N.W., Washington, D.C. 20007; (202) 337–0311.
◆ Big Wheel Bikes, 1034 Thirty-third Street N.W., Washington, D.C. 20007; (202) 337–0254.

MAPS

◆ *ADC's Washington Area Bike Map.* Compiled by Metropolitan Washington Council of Governments. $10.95. Available at bookstores and newsstands.
◆ *D.C. Bikeways.* Series of maps published by the city. $3.00. Write to District of Columbia Office of Documents, 441 Fourth Street N.W., Suite 520, Washington, D.C. 20001; (202) 727–5090.
◆ *Maryland Bicycle Touring Map.* Free. Available from Office of Tourism Development, 45 Calvert Street, Annapolis, MD 21401.
◆ *Trails in Montgomery County Parks.* Contact Maryland–National Capital Park and Planning Commission (MNCPPC), 8787 Georgia Avenue N.W., Silver Spring, MD 20910; (301) 495–2503; www.mncppc.org.

Three-State Special Cruise

I f all cyclists were like David Brown, books like this would never be published. Mr. Brown, a Washington lawyer, owns a weekend house in Round Hill, Virginia, 5 miles from the end of the W & OD Trail. With a detailed Virginia map in hand, he started creating his own bike routes that include historic and scenic areas of Virginia, West Virginia, and Maryland. My great thanks to him for sharing his two favorites, which I've combined here into one long ride.

Many of the roads are quiet and little traveled. Just to the west is an apple-growing region. The busier routes feature wide shoulders. The two Potomac crossings can be made on safe bridges. By turning around at South Mountain Natural Area in Maryland, you can shave about one-fifth the distance from the ride.

The ride cuts a swath between the Blue Ridge and Short Hill Mountains. It also takes you through the towns of Hillsboro, Virginia; Sharpsburg, Maryland; Brunswick, Maryland; and Lovettsville, Virginia. As a bicyclist, you'll appreciate riding through Hillsboro, where a historic marker notes this is the birthplace of Susan Koerner Wright, mother of bicycle builders and pioneer aviators Wilbur and Orville Wright. Located in Washington County, Brunswick was once a thriving railroad town, with more than 1,300 people working for the B & O system. Much of its gritty heritage survives, along with a few trains carrying commuters to Washington. Its old houses are arranged in a cozy grid in the shadow of the Catoctin Mountains.

Not far from David Brown's weekend retreat, the area around the confluence of the Shenandoah and the Potomac Rivers was hotly contested during the Civil War. Abolitionist John Brown's raid on Harpers Ferry helped precipitate the conflict. In 1862 Stonewall Jackson captured the town, much to the embarrassment of Abraham Lincoln. Today most of the town has been preserved as a national park, with shops and historic exhibits installed in the old buildings. Founded in 1733, the town offers views of the surrounding rivers and mountains. (Thomas Jefferson called the vista of the two rivers meeting "one of the most stupendous scenes in nature.")

THE BASICS

Start: Purcellville
Distance: 65-mile loop
Approximate pedaling time: 6 hours
Terrain and surface: Hilly; back roads and two-laners with wide shoulders.
Things to see: Antietam Battlefield, Harpers Ferry National Historic Park, farmland
Traffic and hazards: Traffic is light, but it's usually fast moving, so stick to the shoulders; the rolling hills may impede your visibility to drivers
Getting there: By bicycle, take W & OD Trail to end at Purcellville. By auto, take Route 7 west.

If you take the detour to visit historic Harpers Ferry, you also might be attracted by the markers on Trego Road toward John Brown's farm, Kennedy Farmhouse. Recently restored by the National Park Service, this is the site where Brown and others collected arms and ammunition for months prior to their raid on the arsenal in 1859.

Just to the north, Antietam National Battlefield Park commemorates the war's bloodiest day of fighting. On September 17, 1862, some 23,000 of the blue and gray soldiers were killed or wounded. The battle ended in a draw, with the southerners denied the tactical victory they hoped would end the war. The 6.5-mile one-way loop around the park is perfect for cyclists—providing they are feeling reverent. The last time I was there, a group of Civil War re-enactors, authentically dressed down to their eyeglasses, were solemnly setting up camp and preparing artillery as though they were about to charge into battle. They were living in old canvas tents and stoking pit fires, for this was November.

Other highlights of an Antietam tour include the West Woods, where Union forces lost 2,200 troops in thirty minutes; the homespun Dunker Church on disputed high ground; and Bloody Lane, no explanation needed. On the much less grisly side, you can turn off Route 65 for a visit to the Piper Farmhouse, General Longstreet's headquarters during the battle. The 1843 log structure was recently restored as a bed-and-breakfast with kitchen privileges and reasonable rates. Staying overnight (301–797–1862) will give you more time to explore the upper reaches of the C & O Canal and, just across the river, the college burg of Shepardstown, West Virginia, which once thrived on mills and now thrives on antiques.

Antietam's historic sites are all mixed in with private farms and houses. This has caused some alarm, as preservationists charge that development will ruin this hallowed ground. So the battle for Antietam Creek has not been decided yet.

This is the halfway point on this long ride, and you might have worked up a cyclist's appetite before your return. As you ride on Route 34 through Keedysville, you will pass a favorite carbo-loading spot of local cyclists, the Red Byrd Restaurant. Be sure to order a slice of fresh fruit pie—you've earned it!

The region is fewer than 60 miles from central Washington, D.C., but at times it seems several worlds away. At least once a year the Potomac Area Chapter of American Youth Hostels sponsors guided rides out to Harpers Ferry. It's the easiest way I know of to cycle through three states in one day.

LOCAL INFORMATION

♦ Arlington Chamber of Commerce, 2009 Fourteenth Street North, Suite 111, Arlington, VA 22201; (703) 525–2400.
♦ Arlington Convention and Visitors Service, 1100 North Glebe Road, Suite 1500, Arlington, VA 22201; (703) 228–0888 or (800) 677–6267.
♦ Loudoun Convention and Visitors Association, 108-D South Street, Leesburg, VA 20175; (800) 752–6118.

LOCAL EVENTS/ATTRACTIONS

♦ Annual Waterford Homes Tour and Crafts Exhibit, First weekend in October; (540) 882–3085.
♦ Antietam National Battlefield Park, P.O. Box 158, Sharpsburg, MD 21782; (301) 432–5124; www.nps.gov/anti.
♦ Harpers Ferry National Historic Park, P.O. Box 65, Harpers Ferry, WV 25425; (304) 535–6298; www.nps.gov/hafe.

RESTAURANTS

♦ Lost Dog Cafe, Westover Shopping Center, 5876 North Washington Boulevard, Arlington, VA; (703) 237–1552. Probably the best place in town.
♦ Candelora's at the Purcellville Inn, 36855 West Main Street, Purcellville, VA; (540) 338–2075. An Italian restaurant in a restored inn.

ACCOMMODATIONS

♦ Georges Mill Farm B&B, 11867 Georges Mill Road, Lovettsville, VA 20180; (540) 822–5224.

Rolling hills on quiet roads

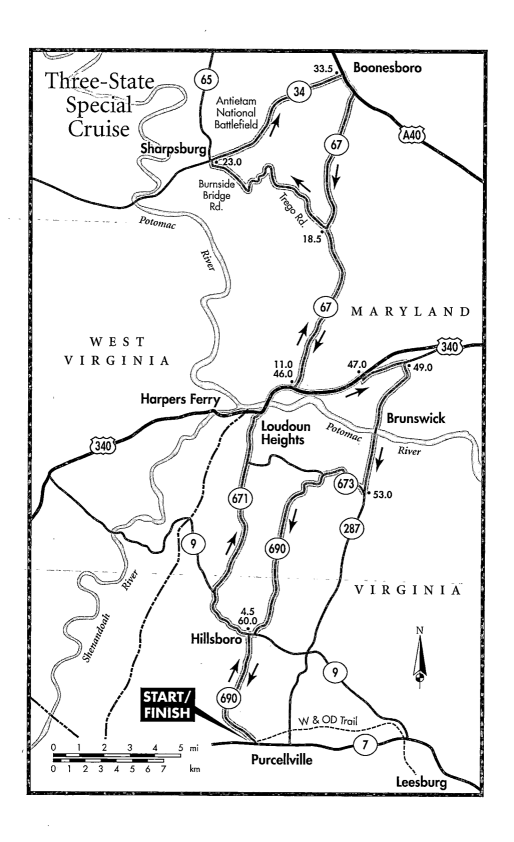

Three-State Special Cruise

Boonesboro

65

Antietam National Battlefield

34

33.5

A40

67

Sharpsburg

• 23.0

Burnside Bridge Rd.

Trego Rd.

18.5

Potomac

River

67

MARYLAND

WEST VIRGINIA

340

11.0
46.0

47.0

• 49.0

Harpers Ferry

Loudoun Heights

Potomac

Brunswick

River

340

673

• 53.0

671

287

9

690

VIRGINIA

Shenandoah

River

4.5
60.0

Hillsboro

N

9

START/ FINISH

690

W & OD Trail

7

0   1   2   3   4   5 mi

0 1 2 3 4 5 6 7   km

Purcellville

Leesburg

Note: Follow directions for the Sharpsburg section carefully; not every small street is shown on the map.

0.0 From Twenty-first Street in Purcellville (end of W & OD Trail), head north on Route 690.

4.5 Near town of Hillsboro, Route 690 comes to T. Turn left onto Route 9.

6.0 Second right onto Route 671.

10.0 Head north to Loudoun Heights, Virginia. Cross Potomac on bridge. Road merges with Route 340 in Maryland (four lanes with wide shoulders).

11.0 Right onto Route 340 north.

Option (Trip to Harpers Ferry, West Virginia): Left on Route 340 to historic park (about 2 miles). Double back to rejoin ride at Route 67.

12.0 Bear right off Route 340 to Route 67 toward Boonesboro. Pass by towns of Garretts Mill, August, Yarrowsburg, and Gapland, to South Mountain Natural Area.

18.5 Left onto Trego Road (becomes Mt. Briar Road).

Option (Trip to John Brown's Farm): Left at marker to Kennedy Farm, John Brown's home, then return to route; 9 miles round trip.

20.0 Left onto Porterstown Road.

23.0 At T intersection, left onto Route 34 (busy with shoulder).

24.5 Ride through town of Sharpsburg; right onto Route 65.

26.0 Right off Route 65 to battlefield visitor center.

Option (8.5-mile tour of battlefield—details at visitor center): From visitor center, left onto Route 65 to turn back.

27.5 Left onto Route 34, through Keedysville. Ride into town of Boonesboro.

33.5 At traffic light, right onto Alternate Route 40 east.

33.75 Right onto Route 67 south.

46.0 Take Route 67 to Route 340. Turn left to head east.

46.5 Right onto Route 180.

47.0 Bear right onto Route 478.

49.0 Just before bridge, turn left onto Virginia Avenue, then immediately right onto West B Street.

50.0 At flashing light, right onto Route 17 and cross bridge over Potomac to Virginia (Route 17 becomes Route 287 south).

53.0 Right onto Route 673.

54.0 Left onto Route 690.

60.0 Near Hillsboro, right onto Route 9.

60.5 Left onto Route 690 to Purcellville.

◆ Piper House Bed & Breakfast, 5537 Sharpsburg Pike, Sharpsburg, MD 21782; (301) 797–1862.

BIKE SHOPS

◆ Revolution Cycles, 2731 Wilson Boulevard, Arlington, VA 22201; (703) 312–0007.
◆ Trailside Bicycles, 201 North Twenty-first Street, Purcellville, VA 20132; (540) 338–4687.

MAPS

◆ *W & OD R.R. Regional Park Trail Guide*. $5.95. Contact Northern Virginia Regional Park Authority, 5400 Ox Road, Fairfax Station, VA 22039; (703) 352–5900. Also available from the W & OD Trail office at (703) 729–0596 and some bike shops.
◆ *Arlington, Virginia, Bikeway Map and Guide*. Published by the Arlington County Department of Public Works. Free. Contact Public Works Planning Division, No. 1 Court House Plaza, 2100 North Clarendon Boulevard, Arlington, VA 22201; (703) 228–3681.
◆ *Virginia Atlas and Gazetteer*. Published by DeLorme Mapping Company. Includes topographic maps, hike/bike trails, canoeing areas. $12.95. Available at bookstores.
◆ *ADC's Washington Area Bike Map*. Compiled by Metropolitan Washington Council of Governments. $10.95. Available at bookstores and newsstands.
◆ *D.C. Bikeways*. Series of maps published by the city. $3.00. Write to District of Columbia Office of Documents, 441 Fourth Street N.W., Suite 520, Washington, D.C. 20001; (202) 727–5090.

Hardly Hilly Hunt
Country Cruise

T he historic small town of Middleburg is the center of Virginia's Hunt Country, one of the most beautiful cycling spots I know. The natural splendor of this area and an interest in the equestrian life have drawn many of America's privileged to call this home. Current and former residents include philanthropist Paul Mellon, actor Robert Duvall, television personality Willard Scott, diplomats Averill and Pamela Harriman, General George S. Patton, and Redskins owner Jack Kent Cooke. President and Jacqueline Kennedy built their home, Wexford, nearby. Wexford was later rented to Ronald and Nancy Reagan by the then current owner while they awaited the inauguration. All this means is that we have an extraordinarily beautiful area to enjoy, simply for the pedaling effort!

Middleburg is so small that it has only *one* stoplight, in front of the Red Fox Inn—the oldest continuously operated inn in America. Founded by Joseph Chinn in 1731, the "ordinary" provided respite for horseback travelers. In 1747 a young surveyor, George Washington, stayed at the Red Fox when employed by Lord Fairfax to survey the surrounding lands. For years the town was known as Chinn's Crossing, but it was renamed Middleburgh (the *h* was later dropped) by Leven Powell in 1787, reflecting the fact that the town was halfway between Alexandria and Winchester, the Shenandoah town then at the edge of the western frontier.

Hunt Country rolling hills

Your first stop might be the Pink House, the visitor center on Madison Street. They can provide you with a walking-tour brochure featuring many of the important houses and churches built in the eighteenth and nineteenth centuries. After your bike ride, I suggest you walk around Middleburg and especially to Sharon Cemetery, a peaceful and contemplative place where Union and Confederate soldiers are buried side by side.

First, a note about the cycling in this area, and this ride in particular. Virginia Hunt Country is not flat; it is rolling to hilly. Few hills are long, but some can be steep. A "granny gear" is standard equipment for many local cyclists. But, believe me, it's worth the added effort to ride in these parts. Every weekend cyclists can be seen on most of these roads. I put this ride together because so many of my friends wanted to ride in Hunt/Horse Country but were concerned that it was too hilly. This ride takes the least hilly roads I could link together. It's not flat, just "hardly hilly."

Be sure to take an extra water bottle; the little country stores that used to dot this area have been closing rapidly. Ride away from Middleburg westward on Route 50, also known as the John S. Mosby Highway. You'll be riding toward Mount Defiance on the same route Union troops took into the Battle of Middleburg in July 1863. Turn left on Zulla Road, where you'll pass the first of many horse farms. Off to the right, you'll have sweeping views of the Blue Ridge Mountains. In spring, dogwoods and redbud are plentiful along this road; in the fall, the foliage colors are stunning.

Along the Atoka Road, you'll pass Kent Farms, the residence and horse stables of the late Jack Kent Cooke, owner of the Redskins football team. Nearby, the Kent Polo Grounds can be found off Route 624 where polo is played every Sunday afternoon during summer months. Shortly, you'll pass Atoka Farms, a previous estate of Senator John Warner. Cross busy Route 50 and continue on St. Louis Road past Notre Dame Academy. Once a private school for young ladies from wealthy families, it is now coeducational and has a more egalitarian student body.

When you reach the intersection of Foxcroft and Mountville Roads, notice the house off to your right just down Pothouse Road. Known as The Pot

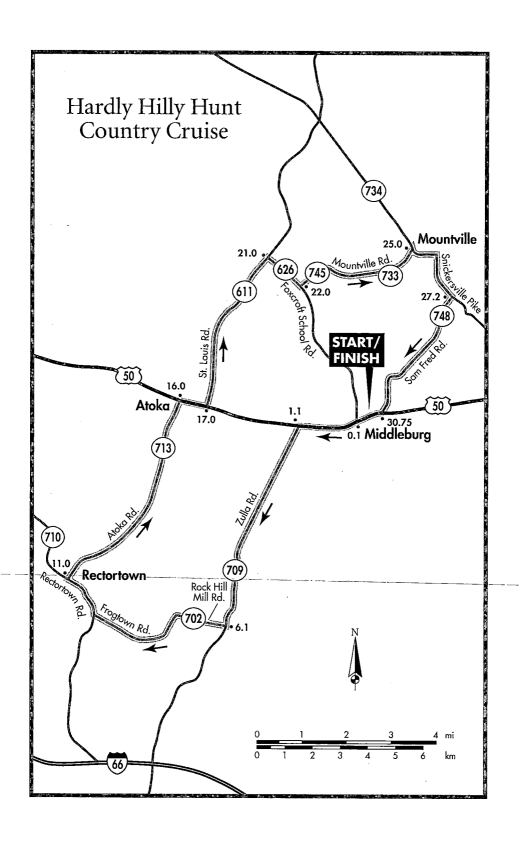

Hardly Hilly Hunt
Country Cruise

734

25.0 · **Mountville**

21.0 ·

626 745 *Mountville Rd.* 733

611 *Foxcroft School Rd.* · 22.0

27.2 ·

748

Snickersville Pike

**START/
FINISH**

50

16.0 ·

Atoka

17.0 ·

· 1.1

30.75 ·
0.1 **Middleburg**
· 0.1

50

Sam Fred Rd.

St. Louis Rd.

713

Atoka Rd.

Zulla Rd.

710

11.0 ·

Rectortown

709

Rock Hill
Mill Rd.

Rectortown Rd.

Froglown Rd.

702 · 6.1

N

66

| 0 | 1 | 2 | 3 | 4 mi |
| 0 | 1 2 | 3 4 | 5 | 6 km |

0.0 Left out of school lot back onto Route 626.

0.1 Right onto Route 50 through Middleburg.

1.1 Left onto Zulla Road, Route 709.

6.1 Right onto Route 702, Rock Hill Mill Road (easy to miss). Bear left on Route 710; becomes Frogtown Road. At T intersection, right onto Route 710, Rectortown Road.

11.0 Right onto Atoka Road, Route 713.

16.0 Right onto Route 50 (shoulder).

17.0 Left onto St. Louis Road, Route 611.

21.0 Right onto Foxcroft School Road, Route 626.

22.0 Left onto Route 745, Mountville Road.

23.0 Bear right on Route 733.

25.0 In Mountville, right onto Route 734, Snickersville Pike. Bear right to remain on Snickersville Pike at Route 773.

27.2 Right onto Sam Fred Road, Route 748.

30.75 Right onto Route 50 (busy; stay right).

31.25 Right at stoplight, back to school parking lot.

House, pottery for local farmers was made here for nearly a century after 1795. As you ride along Mountville Road (one of my favorites) be on the lookout for white-tail deer or a red fox. I rarely come down this road without sighting one or the other. The ride ends with an easy ride down Sam Fred Road, intersecting with busy Route 50. Be sure to stay to the right on Route 50; the trucks and cars should be slowing down as they approach Middleburg, but they still can be quite fast.

LOCAL INFORMATION

♦ Town of Middleburg, 10 West Marshall Street, P.O. Box 187, Middleburg, VA 20118-0187; (540) 687–5152.

LOCAL EVENTS / ATTRACTIONS

♦ Virginia Fall Races, Glenwood Park, P.O. Box 2, Middleburg, VA 20118; (540) 687–5662.

♦ Delaplane Strawberry Festival, Sky Meadows State Park (Route 17 just south of Route 50); Sky Meadows State Park: (540) 592–3556; Piedmont Parish: (540) 364–2772. Late May; $15 per car.

ACCOMMODATIONS

◆ Red Fox Inn, 2 East Washington Street, Middleburg, VA 20117; (540) 687–6301.

◆ Middleburg Country Inn, 209 East Washington Street, Middleburg, VA 20117; (540) 687–6082.

◆ Briar Patch Bed & Breakfast, 23120 Briar Patch Lane, Middleburg, VA 20117; (703) 327–5911 or (866) 327–5911; www.bbonline.com/va/briarpatch.

MAPS

◆ *Virginia Atlas and Gazetteer.* Published by DeLorme Mapping Company. Includes topographic maps, hike/bike trails, canoeing areas. $12.95. Available at bookstores.

◆ *ADC's Washington Area Bike Map.* Compiled by Metropolitan Washington Council of Governments. $10.95. Available at bookstores and newsstands.

Winery and Woods Cruise

This cruise will take you through picturesque views of endless fields and English rock walls; over rolling hills and around tall, wooden barns. Keep to the edges of the roads to be on the safe side, but traffic here is far more courteous than in the city. You will find yourself pedaling strongly to get over some of the hills and feel the wind racing through your hair on the downhill.

This ride also begins at Middleburg, described in Ride 27. The Civil War left many marks on Middleburg and surrounding villages. Its proximity to Washington placed it where guerrilla actions by Confederate troops frequently occurred. These were the stomping grounds of General John S. Mosby, the "Gray Ghost." The townspeople voted unanimously for secession, sympathized with the Southern Cause, and provided food, shelter, and hiding places for many of Mosby's Rangers. It is said that Mosby himself was hidden for several days in a house still standing on the eastern edge of town, while Union troops searched unsuccessfully as the owners steadfastly denied knowing his whereabouts. The town's residents paid dearly for their allegiance, however; Union troops frequently took horses and other provisions whenever needed—and hauled the few remaining men off to prison in Washington.

The only major battle fought here was about a mile out of town, the Battle of Middleburg. General J.E.B. Stuart was informed that Union troops were traveling westward on Little River Turnpike (now Route 50) toward Ashby's Gap. Initially, he sought to hold them back at Aldie, but he was unsuccessful and fell back to Mount Defiance just outside Middleburg for another stand. Both sides lost many men, but the Union army was eventually successful and went on to capture Upperville and Ashby's Gap. Nearly 2,000 men were lost between the armies; many are buried together in Sharon Cemetery.

Middleburg was largely impoverished after the Civil War, with crops destroyed, horses taken, few able men, and no money to hire farmhands. Houses and farms deteriorated, but fortunately were not destroyed. As the fortunes of Americans grew, they sought open fields for their estates and their newfound interest in horses and foxhunting. The vast, rolling terrain provided the perfect environment for these sports—and for grapes.

Wine has been produced in America since colonial times. The Virginia General Assembly sought to encourage a native wine industry by its "Act for the Encouragement of the Making of Wine" in 1769, but poor luck in the vineyards and the Revolution interrupted efforts. In the nineteenth century, wine production again flourished in Virginia after a local variety, named Norton for its discoverer, was found to survive. Then came Prohibition, all but terminating the industry.

Viniculture slowly recovered in the mid–twentieth century. American and French vines were grafted together to combine the finesse of vinifera wines with the hardiness and resistance to phylloxera of the native species. By the 1970s, viticultural research and development had made commercial farm wine

Middleburg Elementary School

production possible in Virginia. Mrs. Thomas Elizabeth Furness started the first commercial vineyard in Virginia since colonial times at Piedmont Vineyards in 1973, just south of Middleburg. This bicycle tour takes you by this vineyard, then adds another loop through wonderful, wooded territory north of town.

This is a figure-eight tour, and you could take either loop first. I suggest that you first ride the southern one, as it is hillier and you'll be less tempted to call it a day when you loop back through Middleburg for the second loop. Ride west through Middleburg, and head south on The Plains Road. This is the same road where Union and

Confederate cavalries clashed. You are at a high point now, and the views right and left are spectacular. After cruising downhill, you'll encounter Piedmont Vineyards, with its stately mansion, Waverly, prominently facing the road. The house was begun in 1755 and finally restored in 1942, after it had fallen on hard times during the early 1900s. In 2002 Piedmont Vineyards remodeled a 1915 stable to be its new tasting room, with a 24-foot copper bar and a fireplace. They have also placed picnic tables outside that are available all year. Tours and tastings are available most days (540–687–5528).

Don't linger there long, however. You have several more miles of countryside to enjoy. Continue on The Plains Road to Halfway, so named because it was the midpoint between Middleburg and The Plains, where the train stopped.

You'll return to Middleburg's stoplight; cross over Route 50 past your starting point, and head north on Foxcroft School Road. Turn right at The Pot House, described in Ride 27, along Mountville Road, canopied by trees in many places. At Snickersville Turnpike, which is a Virginia Scenic Byway, turn right, passing stables and stone fences through winding, wooded roads. Be alert for deer here; I've had a few close calls with those bounding whitetails along this road. Now circle back to Middleburg, pick up your car, and drive back to the winery to pick up a few bottles!

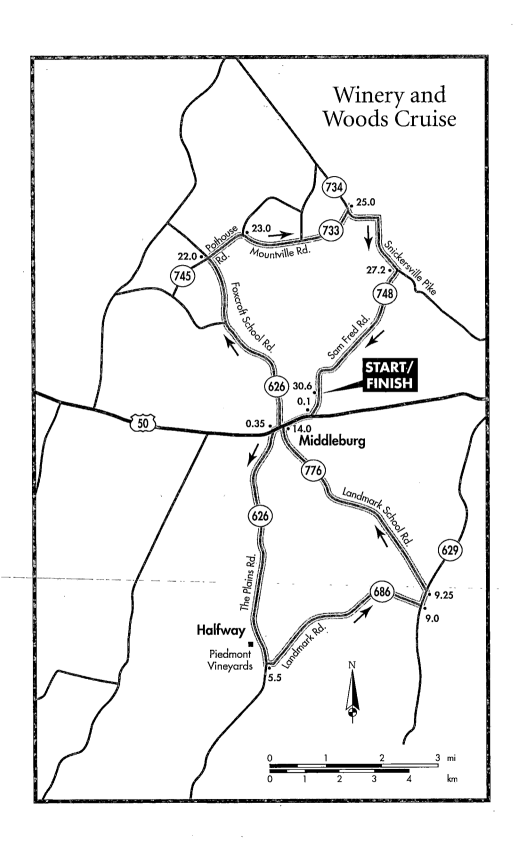

Winery and Woods Cruise

734
• 25.0

733
23.0 →
↓

Pothouse
Rd.

22.0 •
Mountville Rd.
Snickersville Pike

745
27.2 •

Foxcroft School Rd.
748

Sam Fred Rd.
↙

626 30.6
↗
**START/
FINISH**

0.1 •

50
0.35 •
• 14.0
Middleburg

↙
776

626
Landmark School Rd.
↖

629

The Plains Rd.
686
• 9.25

Halfway
↗
• 9.0

Piedmont
Vineyards
Landmark Rd.

• 5.5
N

0		1		2		3	mi
0	1	2	3	4			km

0.0 From the school parking lot, turn left to Route 50 stoplight.

0.1 Right onto Route 50 through Middleburg.

0.35 Left on The Plains Road, Route 626.

5.5 Hard left at Halfway onto Landmark Road. At Route 679, bear left to remain on Landmark Road.

9.0 Left onto Route 629.

9.25 Left onto Landmark School Road, Route 776.

14.0 Cross Route 50 at stoplight and straight onto Foxcroft School Road, past starting point. Bear right to remain on Foxcroft Road at Snake Hill.

22.0 Right onto Mountville Road, Route 745.

23.0 Bear right onto Route 733, Mountville Road.

25.0 In Mountville, right onto Route 734, Snickersville Pike.

25.5 Bear right to remain on Snickersville Pike at Route 773.

26.1 Turn right (second right-hand turn) and stay on Snickersville Turnpike; Route 734—if you continue, you'll pass Lime Kiln Road and need to turn back.

27.2 Right onto Sam Fred Road, Route 748.

30.6 Right onto Route 50 (busy; stay right).

31.3 Right at stoplight back to school parking lot.

LOCAL INFORMATION

♦ Town of Middleburg, 10 West Marshall Street, P.O. Box 187, Middleburg, VA 20118-0187; (540) 687–5152.

LOCAL EVENTS/ATTRACTIONS

♦ Virginia Fall Races, Glenwood Park, P.O. Box 2, Middleburg, VA 20118; (540) 687–5662.

♦ Delaplane Strawberry Festival, Sky Meadows State Park (Route 17 just south of Route 50); Sky Meadows State Park: (540) 592–3556; Piedmont Parish: (540) 364–2772. Late May; $15 per car.

ACCOMMODATIONS

♦ Red Fox Inn, 2 East Washington Street, Middleburg, VA 20117; (540) 687–6301.

♦ Middleburg Country Inn, 209 East Washington Street, Middleburg VA 20117; (540) 687–6082.

♦ Briar Patch Bed & Breakfast, 23130 Briar Patch Lane, Middleburg, VA 20117; (703) 327–5911 or (866) 327–5911; www.bbonline.com/va/briarpatch.

MAPS

♦ *Virginia Atlas and Gazetteer.* Published by DeLorme Mapping Company. Includes topographic maps, hike/bike trails, canoeing areas. $12.95. Available at bookstores.

♦ *ADC's Washington Area Bike Map.* Compiled by Metropolitan Washington Council of Governments. $10.95. Available at bookstores and newsstands.

Blue Ridge Splendor Cruise

T his 41-mile cruise will bring you close to the Blue Ridge
Mountains, past stables and foxhunting country, steeplechase
tracks, and gorgeous stone homes. The terrain is certainly rolling and
hilly, but on a sunny day with a gentle breeze this ride can be as much
of a pleasure cruise as a workout.

The Blue Ridge Mountains lie to the west, creating a challenge for cyclists
wishing to ride to the Shenandoah Valley. This ride takes us westward far
enough to enjoy the mountains' spectacular beauty without tackling their
inclines. This ride is particularly colorful in fall, but I enjoy riding it any time
of the year. In fact, it's my favorite ride in the Virginia Hunt Country.

Part of the Appalachians, the Blue Ridge Mountains are some of the oldest eastern mountains. Geologists now believe they once were much larger—
towering higher than the Rockies eons ago. However, thousands of years of
rain, wind, ice, and weathering smoothed the once snowcapped peaks to
today's rolling ridges. The dense hardwood forests provide great hiking opportunities and beautiful foliage. From afar, the mountains are striking as the sunlight, cloud shadows, and haze create unending variations of panoramic display.

Along the way, you'll pass several points of interest reflecting the residents'
long-standing interest in horses, including foxhunting, horse shows, racing,
and polo. Riding north on Foxcroft School Road, you'll pass Glenwood Park,
where both point-to-point and steeplechase races are run. Yes, there are differ-
ences between the two: largely whether timber or brush fences are to be
jumped, whether professionals are allowed to compete, and the size or absence
of a purse. However, efforts to make the races more accessible for spectators
have tended to limit the rambling point-to-points to a smaller field, making

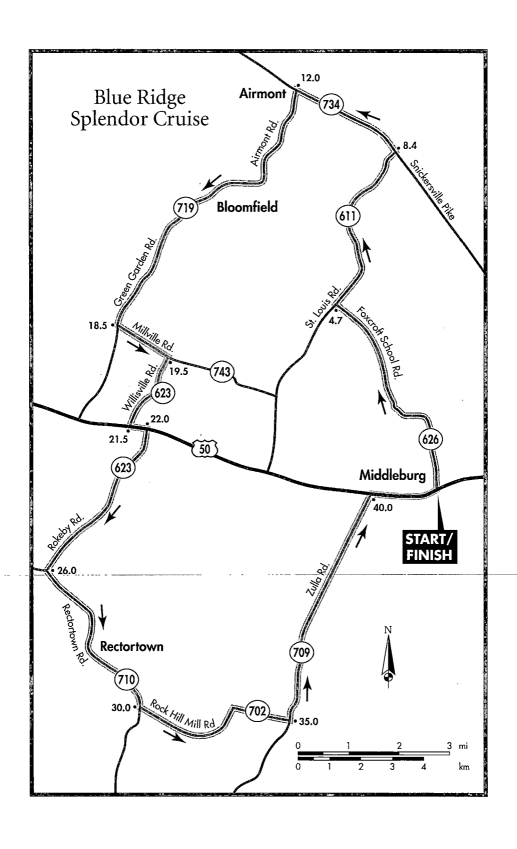

Blue Ridge
Splendor Cruise

Airmont

12.0

734

8.4

Snickersville Pike

Airmont Rd.

719   Bloomfield

611

Green Garden Rd.

St. Louis Rd.

4.7

Foxcroft School Rd.

18.5

Millville Rd.

19.5   743

Willisville Rd.

623

22.0

623

21.5

50

626

Middleburg

40.0

Rokeby Rd.

26.0

Zulla Rd.

START/
FINISH

Rectortown Rd.

Rectortown

709

710

30.0

Rock Hill Mill Rd

702

35.0

N

0	1	2	3 mi
0	1 2	3	4 km

them more like a steeplechase. For most, either will be equally enjoyable, especially if you just happen to ride by as one is under way.

After passing Glenwood Park, you'll go down a fairly steep hill. About midway, on the left, notice the metal sign featuring a fox. This is the home of the Middleburg Hunt; you may hear the baying of foxhounds in the distance. Don't worry, I've never been chased by a pack of hounds on this road. Foxhunting was brought to America by the British, perhaps as long ago as the late 1600s. Unlike opossums or squirrels, foxes are crafty and put up quite a chase. Foxes were so important to expanding the sport, they were imported from England so that they could mix with the indigenous breed and expand their numbers. In America, the fox is rarely killed; the chase is the sport, requiring excellent horsemanship, good hounds, and a well-trained mount.

THE BASICS

Start: Middleburg Elementary School
Distance: 41 miles
Approximate pedaling time: 3 hours
Terrain and surface: Rolling to hilly; paved two-lane roads
Things to see: Views of Blue Ridge Mountains, stables
Traffic and hazards: Light traffic
Facilities: Stores in Middleburg, Bloomfield
Getting there: Take Route 66 west to Route 50 (exit 57). Follow Route 50 for approximately 20 miles to town of Middleburg. Turn right at only stoplight onto Route 626, Foxcroft School Road. Park in elementary school lot.

MILES AND DIRECTIONS

0.0 Turn right onto Foxcroft School Road, Route 626, from the school parking lot. Continue straight at Pot House Road.

4.7 Right onto Route 611, St. Louis Road.

8.4 Left at blinking light, Route 734.

12.0 Left onto Airmont Road, Route 719. *Note:* Airmont Road becomes Green Garden Road.

18.5 Left onto Millville Road, Route 743.

19.5 Bear right on Route 623, Willisville Road.

21.5 Left onto Route 50 (traffic).

22.0 Right onto Route 623, Rokeby Road.

26.0 Left at T onto Rectortown Road, Route 710.

30.0 Rectortown Road, Route 710, changes at Frogtown to Frogtown Road, Route 702. Bear right still on Route 702, which becomes Rock Hill Mill Road.

35.0 Left onto Zulla Road, Route 709.

40.0 Right onto Route 50.

41.0 Left at stoplight back to parking lot.

After turning south at Airmont, you'll have the Blue Ridge Mountains on your right for several miles. Periodically glance over and see how they change as the sunlight shifts. As you cross Route 50, you'll be at Grafton Farm, site of the Upperville Colt and Horse Show, the nation's oldest horse show. Since 1853, interrupted only during war years, this show has featured young colts and fillies, usually raised nearby. While the show was founded to encourage production of top breeding stock, other classes have been added over the years to round out horsemen's interests. The show has grown so much that events now last the first full week of June and occupy fields on both sides of Route 50. The High Jump became a major attraction; recently commercialism has taken hold with the Michelob-Upperville Jumper Classic, featuring a very sizable purse.

On Rokeby Road, you'll pass the estate of philanthropist Paul Mellon. Shortly after passing the airstrip on your right, look left and you'll see the roofline of the stables. This is the home of some of Virginia's best thoroughbreds. In addition to the real horseflesh, these stables contain life-size bronze statues of Mill Reef and Kentucky Derby winner Sea Hero. Completing the loop, you'll ride through Rectortown and pass close by yet another horse-oriented sport venue, the Kent Polo Field, on your left down graveled Crenshaw Road. Polo is played here every Sunday afternoon during summer. If horses really interest you, you might want to take in the annual Stable Tour, held every Memorial Day weekend, when you can visit Rokeby as well as other private stables and stud farms.

LOCAL INFORMATION

♦ Town of Middleburg, 10 West Marshall Street, P.O. Box 187, Middleburg, VA 20118-0187; (540) 687–5152

LOCAL EVENTS/ATTRACTIONS

♦ Virginia Fall Races, Glenwood Park, P.O. Box 2, Middleburg, VA 20118; (540) 687–5662.
♦ Delaplane Strawberry Festival, Sky Meadows State Park (Route 17 just south of Route 50); Sky Meadows State Park: (540) 592–3556; Piedmont Parish: (540) 364–2772. Late May; $15 per car.

ACCOMMODATIONS

♦ Red Fox Inn, 2 East Washington Street, Middleburg VA 20117; (540) 687–6301.
♦ Middleburg Country Inn, 209 East Washington Street, Middleburg, VA 20117; (540) 687–6082.

◆ Briar Patch Bed & Breakfast, 23130 Briar Patch Lane, Middleburg, VA 20117; (703) 327–5911 or (866) 327–5911; www.bbonline.com/va/briarpatch.

MAPS

◆ *Virginia Atlas and Gazetteer.* Published by DeLorme Mapping Company. Includes topographic maps, hike/bike trails, canoeing areas. $12.95. Available at bookstores.
◆ *ADC's Washington Area Bike Map.* Compiled by Metropolitan Washington Council of Governments. $10.95. Available at bookstores and newsstands.

To the Races Cruise

his ride takes you to the site of Virginia's premier steeplechase event, The Virginia Gold Cup. Along the way you'll have great views of the Blue Ridge Mountains, see some Texas longhorns, and visit at the site of the former railroad stop that bypassed Middleburg, fueling Middleburg's earlier decline.

The Virginia Gold Cup, held the first Saturday in May, is so important to the local steeplechase circuit that other races are held based on the number of weekends between them and the premier event. For example, steeplechase races at Middleburg's Glenwood Park are held five Saturdays before the Virginia Gold Cup.

Rest assured, this is "the place to be" that May weekend if you are interested in steeplechase racing. Of course, if flat racing is your thing, you'll be at the Kentucky Derby, held the same day. The crowd usually stays around Great Meadow until late afternoon to hear the Derby broadcast over the public address system. The day is one of contrasts: elegant, catered banquets for those on Member's Hill; somewhat less lavish railside parties sponsored by corporations, where lobbyists hope to speak with con-

THE BASICS

Start: Middleburg Elementary School
Distance: 25 miles
Approximate pedaling time: 3 hours
Terrain and surface: Rolling to hilly; paved two-lane roads
Things to see: Great Meadow, The Plains
Traffic and hazards: Light traffic
Facilities: Stores in Middleburg and The Plains
Getting there: Take Route 66 west to Route 50 (exit 57). Follow Route 50 for approximately 20 miles to town of Middleburg. Turn right at only stoplight onto Route 626, Foxcroft School Road. Park in elementary school lot.

Taking time to respect those that preceded our wheeled mounts

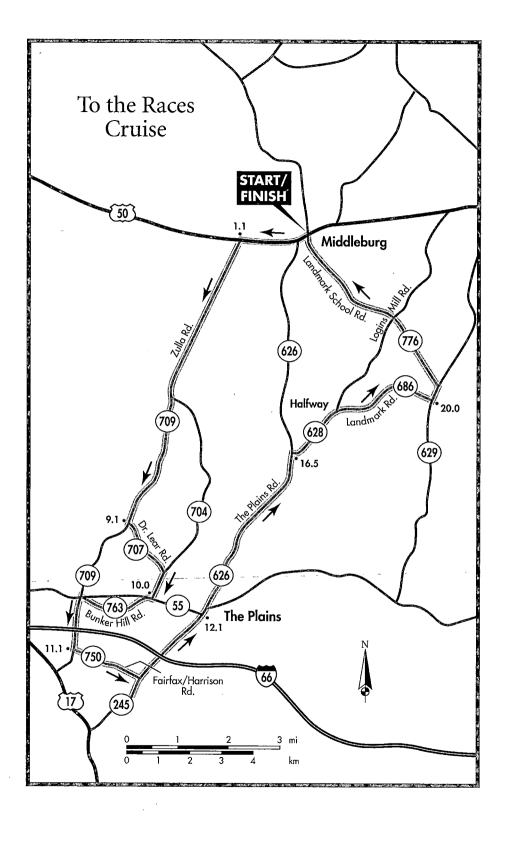

To the Races
Cruise

START/
FINISH

50

1.1

Middleburg

Landmark School Rd.

Logins Mill Rd.

626

776

Halfway

686

709

20.0

628

Landmark Rd.

16.5

629

The Plains Rd.

704

9.1

Dr. Lear Rd.

707

709

626

10.0

763

55

The Plains

Bunker Hill Rd.

12.1

11.1

750

N

Fairfax/Harrison
Rd.

66

17

245

0   1   2   3 mi

0   1   2   3   4   km

0.0 Left out of school lot to stoplight.

0.1 Right onto Route 50 through Middleburg.

1.1 Left onto Zulla Road, Route 709.

9.1 Left onto Route 707, unmarked Dr. Lear Road.

10.0 Right onto Route 55.

10.1 Left onto Bunker Hill Road, Route 763.

11.0 Left onto Route 55; immediate left onto Route 709.

11.1 Left onto Route 750, Fairfax/Harrison Road.

11.2 At T intersection, right onto Route 245 to visit Great Meadow.

11.95 From Great Meadow, turn around and retrace Route 245 to T intersection. Continue on Route 245 into The Plains.

12.1 Left onto Route 55 in The Plains.

12.2 Right onto Route 626.

16.5 At Halfway, right onto Route 679, Landmark Road, toward Picketts Corner.

16.6 Bear left onto Route 628 to remain on Landmark Road. *Note:* Route 628 becomes Logans Mill Road at the 1.4-mile mark from Halfway Road 626. In turn, Landmark Road becomes Route 686.

20.0 Left to remain on Landmark Church Road at Route 629.

20.25 Left onto Landmark School Road, Route 776.

25.0 Cross Route 50 at stoplight and straight onto Foxcroft School Road into parking lot.

gressional bigwigs in a friendly environment; and thousands of everyday horse lovers just out for a day of fun with home-packed picnics and general admission tickets.

The Virginia Gold Cup, around since 1925, has been run near Warrenton most of that time. When its Warrenton home was lost to development, a foundation was formed, Great Meadow was acquired, and the Gold Cup moved there in 1984. The land has a permanent, scenic easement, ensuring a place to enjoy such races in the future. Proceeds from the Gold Cup assist local charities and provide operating expenses so that the land may be used year-round by nonprofit organizations.

As you ride on Route 750 just before Great Meadow, be on the lookout for some Texas longhorns. They are rare in these parts—and an interesting deviation from the horse and cattle farms. After visiting the home of the Gold Cup, ride north through The Plains, where you'll be on nearly flat ground. This is where the railroad line came out from Alexandria. A favorite rest stop of local cyclists here is The Rail Stop, where you can get a bite to eat and a close-up look at a stuffed red fox sitting right in the window.

LOCAL INFORMATION

♦ Town of Middleburg, 10 West Marshall Street, P.O. Box 187, Middleburg, VA 20118-0187; (540) 687–5152

LOCAL EVENTS/ATTRACTIONS

♦ Virginia Fall Races, Glenwood Park, P.O. Box 2, Middleburg, VA 20118; (540) 687–5662.
♦ Delaplane Strawberry Festival, Sky Meadows State Park (Route 17 just south of Route 50); Sky Meadows State Park: (540) 592–3556; Piedmont Parish: (540) 364–2772. Late May; $15 per car.

RESTAURANTS

♦ Red Fox Inn, 2 East Washington Street, Middleburg VA 20117; (540) 687–6301.
♦ Mosby's Tavern, 2 West Marshall Street, Middleburg VA 20117; (540) 687–5282.
♦ Others along the route.

ACCOMMODATIONS

♦ Red Fox Inn, 2 East Washington Street, Middleburg VA 20117; (540) 687–6301.
♦ Middleburg Country Inn, 209 East Washington Street, Middleburg, VA 20117; (540) 687–6082.
♦ Briar Patch Bed & Breakfast. 23130 Briar Patch Lane, Middleburg, VA 20117; (703) 327–5911 or (866) 327–5911; www.bbonline.com/va/briarpatch.

MAPS

♦ *Virginia Atlas and Gazetteer.* Published by DeLorme Mapping Company. Includes topographic maps, hike/bike trails, canoeing areas. $12.95. Available at bookstores.
♦ *ADC's Washington Area Bike Map.* Compiled by Metropolitan Washington Council of Governments. $10.95. Available at bookstores and newsstands.

Historic Waterford Challenge

Although this ride starts from Middleburg, energetic riders seeking to link together several rides and make a long weekend out of touring the Virginia Hunt Country could use the Washington and Old Dominion (W & OD) bike path out to Purcellville and pick up this route, linking it with other rides from Middleburg. There are a few reasonably priced bed-and-breakfast inns near Purcellville, and several more-expensive ones in Middleburg.

The ride takes you through some of Loudoun County's historic towns. The county was formed from Fairfax County and was named for John Campbell, fourth Earl of Loudoun. Although he was named the commander of British forces in North America during an early part of the French and Indian War and was governor of Virginia from 1756 to 1759, he never actually came to the colonies. It was not uncommon for lieutenant governors to be the on-site representatives of nobility, and this was no exception.

On the way, you first pass through Purcellville. This town is west of Leesburg and provided services to travelers on their way to Snickers Gap to reach Winchester or Harpers Ferry. The railroad came in 1874, causing the town to prosper. As you ride along Main Street, you will see many Victorian-style homes resulting from that prosperity.

Arriving in Waterford, note the marker stating that the entire village of Waterford, Virginia, was designated a National Historic Landmark in 1970, one of only three such landmarks in the United States. The village, founded by Quakers from Pennsylvania, was not affected by changing trends or automation, and residents maintained most of their traditional farming methods for many years. As a result, most structures are true to their origins. Limited restoration and preservation is overseen by The Waterford Foundation.

Start: Middleburg Elementary School

Distance: 47 miles

Approximate pedaling time: 4 hours

Terrain and surface: Rolling and hilly; paved two-lane roads, bike paths

Things to see: Historic Waterford and Lincoln

Traffic and hazards: Light traffic

Facilities: Stores in Purcellville, Waterford

Option: Bike out to Purcellville on W & OD path.

Getting there: Take Route 66 west to Route 50 (exit 57). Follow Route 50 for approximately 20 miles to town of Middleburg. Turn right at only stoplight onto Route 626, Foxcroft School Road. Park in elementary school lot.

The Civil War brought strange times to Waterford. Reflecting their Quaker upbringing, most residents were opposed to slavery and voted 221 to 36 against secession. Samuel C. Means, owner of the mill, formed the Loudoun Rangers and led hit-and-run warfare against the Confederates similar to John Mosby's raids against Union troops. The Loudoun Rangers were the only organized unit of Virginians to fight on the side of the Union. Yet, this being Virginia, some locals also joined the Confederacy, leading to one of the more unusual stories of the Civil War.

On August 26, 1862, Means's company arrived at Waterford and occupied the Baptist church. That night they were attacked by part of a Virginia battalion composed of men from Loudoun County. The battle raged for three hours, leaving dead and wounded on both sides. Cease-fires were called twice, and a local woman entered the church to communicate Confederate demands of surrender. Finally, nearly out of ammunition, Means's company surrendered. Despite the surrender, William Snoots, a Confederate soldier, maintained his right to shoot a particular Loudoun Ranger: Charles Snoots, his brother. It took the intervention of a Confederate officer to stop him. Such was the hatred engendered by that war.

Today Waterford is best known for its annual homes tour and craft exhibit, Virginia's oldest juried craft fair, held the first weekend in October. Houses built by Quakers are open for tours, and there is an archaeological display and limited excavation of the late-eighteenth-century tannery operation. This house tour and arts and crafts festival is extremely popular; traffic and parking are terrible. However, I've used this bike route to lead club rides to the fair. Just use Route 704 out and back, and you'll avoid most traffic.

On the return route along the W & OD bike path, you'll pass through Paeonian Springs, which was once a spa. A lake was fed by mineral springs, and the water was shipped all over the United States. The town was named for Paeon Aesculapius, Greek god of medicine. On this section of the bike path, you might sight wild turkeys in spring. If you're riding in fall, keep your eyes open for hairy woodpeckers.

Your next historic town will be Lincoln, another Quaker settlement. The townspeople were historically against slavery, and it is reported that the first meeting of the Manumission and Emigration Society was held here in the Goose Creek schoolhouse as early as 1824. Under the leadership of Yardley Taylor, the community was actively involved with the Underground Railroad.

The return route will follow parts of the Snickersville Turnpike, a winding, narrow road over Hibbs Bridge with stone walls flanking one or both sides. The road is currently designated a Virginia Scenic Byway, and local residents are seeking to increase its preservation status to guard against plans of the Virginia Department of Transportation to widen and straighten it into a commuter route. Proposed changes would eliminate most of its character and some of the centuries-old walls. There is at least one "hill of note" on this road; I'm sure you'll figure out which one I mean!

LOCAL INFORMATION

♦ Town of Middleburg, 10 West Marshall Street, P.O. Box 187, Middleburg, VA 20118-0187; (540) 687–5152.

LOCAL EVENTS/ATTRACTIONS

♦ Virginia Fall Races, Glenwood Park, P.O. Box 2, Middleburg, VA 20118; (540) 687–5662.
♦ Delaplane Strawberry Festival, Sky Meadows State Park (Route 17 just south of Route 50); Sky Meadows State Park: (540) 592–3556; Piedmont Parish: (540) 364–2772. Late May; $15 per car.

ACCOMMODATIONS

♦ Red Fox Inn, 2 East Washington Street, Middleburg VA 20117; (540) 687–6301.
♦ Middleburg Country Inn, 209 East Washington Street, Middleburg, VA 20117; (540) 687–6082.
♦ Briar Patch Bed & Breakfast, 23130 Briar Patch Lane, Middleburg, VA 20117; (703) 327–5911 or (866) 327–5911; www.bbonline.com/va/briarpatch.

MAPS

♦ *Virginia Atlas and Gazetteer.* Published by DeLorme Mapping Company. Includes topographic maps, hike/bike trails, canoeing areas. $12.95. Available at bookstores.
♦ ADC's *Washington Area Bike Map.* Compiled by Metropolitan Washington Council of Governments. $10.95. Available at bookstores and newsstands.

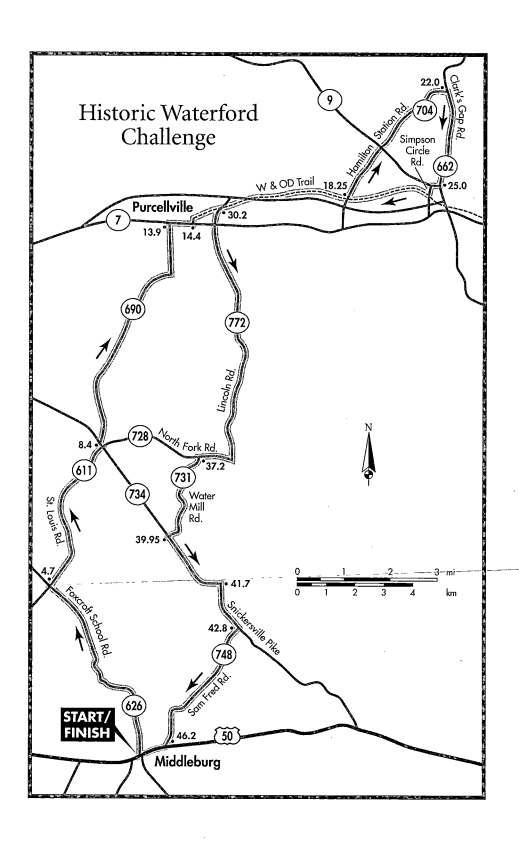

Historic Waterford Challenge

9

22.0

704

Clark's Gap Rd.

Hamilton Station Rd.

Simpson
Circle
Rd.

662

25.0

W & OD Trail 18.25

Purcellville

30.2

7

13.9

14.4

690

772

Lincoln Rd.

728

North Fork Rd.

8.4

37.2

611

731

Water
Mill
Rd.

734

St. Louis Rd.

39.95

4.7

41.7

Foxcroft School Rd.

Snickersville Pike

42.8

748

N

Sam Fred Rd.

626

START/
FINISH

46.2

50

Middleburg

0   1   2   3 mi
0   1   2   3   4   km

0.0 From the school lot, go right onto Foxcroft School Road, Route 626. Straight at Pot House Road.

4.7 Right onto St. Louis Road, Route 611.

8.4 At light, straight onto Route 690 (Route 611 becomes Route 690).

13.9 At T intersection, turn right onto Business Route 7 into Purcellville.

14.4 Left onto Hatcher Avenue.

14.5 Right onto W & OD bike path.

18.25 Left onto Hamilton Station Road, Route 704.

22.0 Right onto Route 662, Clark's Gap Road.

22.25 Left onto Factory Street, into Waterford.

22.5 Return on Factory Street and turn right onto Route 662.

25.0 Right onto Route 9.

25.1 Immediate left onto Simpson Circle Road.

25.2 Right onto W & OD bike path in Paeonian Springs.

30.2 Bear left onto Maple Avenue, Route 722, into Purcellville. Cross Route 7, onto Lincoln Road (still Route 722).

36.45 Right onto North Fork Road, Route 728.

37.2 Left onto Water Mill Road, Route 731.

39.95 Left onto Snickersville Turnpike, Route 734.

41.7 Turn right (fifth right-hand turn) and stay on Snickersville Turnpike, Route 734—if you continue, you will pass Lime Kiln Road and need to turn back.

42.8 Right onto Sam Fred Road, Route 748.

46.2 Right onto Route 50 (busy; stay right).

46.9 Right at stoplight back to school parking lot.

Appendix

BICYCLING ORGANIZATIONS
IN THE D.C. AREA

National Center for Bicycling and Walking
1506 21st Street N.W., Suite 200
Washington, D.C. 20036
(202) 463–6622
www.bikewalk.org
National nonprofit group that promotes safe bicycle use.

League of American Bicyclists
1612 K Street N.W., Suite 401
Washington, D.C. 20006
(202) 822–1333
www.bikeleague.org
The nation's oldest nonprofit organization representing cyclists in the United
States. Sponsors the National Bike Month (May) and founded the
International Police Mountain Bike Association.

Potomac Chapter of American Youth Hostels
1108 K Street N.W.
Washington, D.C. 20005
(202) 783–4943
www.hiayh.org/council/va.htm
Local chapter of national group runs bike trips of one day or more, operates
downtown youth hostel and bike/outdoors shop, plans rides to other hostels
in the region.

Potomac Pedalers Touring Club
6729 Curran Street
McLean, VA 22101
(202) 363–8687
www.cyberider.us.net/bikes/PPTC.html
With more than 4,500 members, the Potomac Pedalers Club is the largest
recreational cycling organization in the Washington area. The group runs
weekly rides and tours, published in their monthly newsletter, *Pedal Patter.*

Washington Area Bicyclist Association
1511 K Street, Suite 1015
Washington, D.C. 20005
(202) 628–2500
www.waba.org
A group that advocates improved trails and routes for bicycle commuters.
Also operates a warehouse for maps and cycling books.

REGIONAL CONSERVATION GROUPS

Audubon Naturalist Society
8940 Jones Mill Road
Chevy Chase, MD 20815
(301) 652–9188
www.audubonnaturalist.org
Local environmental organization that offers many educational programs.

Potomac Appalachian Trail Club
118 Park Street S.E.
Vienna, VA 22180
(703) 242–0315
www.patc.simplenet.com
Local nonprofit group dedicated to creating and preserving hiking trails in
the Mid-Atlantic region.

MAPS TO OBTAIN

ADC's Washington Area Bike Map. Compiled by Metropolitan Washington
Council of Governments. $10.95. Available at bookstores and newsstands.

Arlington, Virginia, Bikeway Map and Guide. Published by the Arlington
County Department of Public Works. Free. Contact Public Works Planning
Division, No. 1 Court House Plaza, 2100 North Clarendon Boulevard,
Arlington, VA 22201; (703) 228–3681.

D.C. Bikeways. Series of eight maps published by the city. $3.00. Write to
District of Columbia Office of Documents, 441 Fourth Street N.W., Suite 520,
Washington, D.C. 20001; (202) 727–5090.

Maryland Bicycle Touring Map. Free. Available from Office of Tourism
Development, 45 Calvert Street, Annapolis, MD 21401.

Station Masters: A Comprehensive Guide to Metrorail Station Neighborhoods.
Published by Bowring Cartographic. $3.95. Available at bookstores.

Trails in Montgomery County Parks. Contact Maryland National Capital Parks and Planning Commission (MNCPPC), 8787 Georgia Avenue N.W., Silver Spring, MD 20910; (301) 495–2503.

Virginia Atlas and Gazetteer. Published by DeLorme Mapping Company. Includes topographic maps, hike/bike trails, canoeing areas. $12.95. Available at bookstores.

Washington, D.C., and Vicinity Street Map. Published by ADC. $9.95. Available at bookstores.

W & OD R.R. Regional Park Trail Guide. $5.95. Contact Northern Virginia Regional Park Authority, 5400 Ox Road, Fairfax Station, VA 22039; (703) 352–5900. Also available from the W & OD Trail office at (703) 729–0596 and some bike shops.

SUGGESTED READING

Abramson, Rudy. *Hallowed Ground: Preserving America's Heritage.* Charlottesville, VA: Thomasson–Grant & Lickle, 1996.

Applewhite, E. J. *Washington, Itself: An Informal Guide to the Capital of the United States.* Second edition. Maryland: Madison Books, 1993.

Bergner, Audrey Windsor. *The Visitor's Guide to Middleburg, Virginia, and the Surrounding John Singleton Mosby Heritage Area.* Virginia: The Middleburg Press, 1997.

Choukas-Bradley, Melanie, and Polly Alexander. *City of Trees: The Complete Field Guide to the Trees of Washington, D.C.* Baltimore: The Johns Hopkins Press, 1987.

Colbert, Judy. *Virginia Off the Beaten Path.* Seventh edition. Guilford, CT: The Globe Pequot Press, 2002.

Hahn, Thomas F. *Towpath Guide to the C & O Canal.* Freemansburg, PA: American Canal and Transport Society, 1996.

Halle, Louis J. *Spring in Washington.* Baltimore: The Johns Hopkins Press, 1988.

Helfer, Chuck, and Gail Helfer. *Chuck and Gail's Favorite Rides.* Takoma Park, MD: Cycleways, 1992.

Scheel, Eugene M. *The History of Middleburg and Vicinity.* Virginia: The Piedmont Press, 1987.

Weeks, Christopher. *AIA Guide to the Architecture of Washington, D.C.* Third edition. Baltimore: The Johns Hopkins Press, 1994.

Wilds, Claudia. *Finding Birds in the National Capital Area.* Washington, D.C.: Smithsonian Institution Press, 1983.

Wurman, Richard Saul. *Washington, D.C. Access: The Capital Guide to the Capital City.* Los Angeles: Access Press, 1989.

BICYCLE RENTAL AND REPAIR CENTERS IN THE D.C. AREA

Big Wheel Bikes. In Georgetown: 1034 Thirty-third Street N.W., Washington, D.C.; (202) 337–0254. On Capitol Hill: 315 Seventh Street S.E., Washington, D.C.; (202) 543–1600. In Old Town: 2 Prince Street, Alexandria, VA; (703) 739–2300. In Bethesda: 6917 Arlington Road, Bethesda, MD; (301) 652–0192. All types of bikes.

City Bikes, 2501 Champlain Street N.W., Washington, D.C.; (202) 265–1564. Mountain bikes and hybrids.

Fletcher's Boat House, 4940 Canal Road N.W., Washington, D.C.; (202) 244–0461. One- and fifteen-speed bikes. Seasonal.

Metropolis Bike & Scooter, Inc. On Capitol Hill: 709 Eighth Street S.E., Washington, D.C.; (202) 543–8900. In Arlington: 4056 South Twenty-eighth Street (The Village at Shirlington), Arlington, VA; (703) 671–1700. ATB and hybrids.

Potomac Outdoors, 7687 MacArthur Boulevard, Cabin John, MD; (301) 320–1544. ATB and hybrids.

Spinnaker 'n' Spoke, at the Washington Sailing Marina (Daingerfield Island), on the Mount Vernon Bike Path; (703) 548–9027. One- and fifteen-speed bikes. Seasonal.

Swain's Lock, about 2.5 miles west of Great Falls on the C & O Canal; (301) 299–9006. One-speed bikes; tandems. Seasonal.

Thompson Boat Center, Rock Creek Parkway & Virginia Avenue N.W., Washington, D.C.; (202) 333–4861. One- and twenty-one-speed bikes, kids' bikes. Seasonal.

Washington Bike Center (Reston Town Center), 11932 Democracy Drive, Reston, VA; (703) 742–7775. Hybrids.

ORGANIZED BIKE RIDES AROUND D.C.

If you prefer riding with lots of other cyclists, there are a number of organized rides near Washington you might wish to join—notably, multiday rides in Maryland and Virginia. These are held annually, with a new route each year. Unfortunately, it isn't safe for large numbers of cyclists to compete with traffic on D.C. roads, so there are few commercial rides actually in D.C.

An exception is Bike the Sites, which leads small groups around the Mall and on the Mount Vernon Trail. Bike rentals are included in the price. Information is available at (202) 966–8662 or www.bikethesites.com.

Bike Virginia organizes a five-day ride through Virginia countryside each year, usually in June. Luggage is transported, and riders may camp or stay in nearby motels. Weekend trips are also held a couple of times a year. Contact (757) 229–0507 or www.bikevirginia.org.

Cycle Across Maryland offers a weeklong ride in a different part of the state each July. Camping or motels are offered. Fat-tire weekends are also arranged. Contact (888) CAM–RIDE or www.cyclexmd.org.

Fund-raising cycle tours of one or two days are organized by the D.C. Multiple Sclerosis Society. Contact (202) 296–5353 or www.dcw.nmss.org. D.C. Habitat for Humanity (202–610–2355) offers a one-day ride. The Maryland Chapter of the MS Society also offers multiday fund-raising rides (800–FIGHT–MS).

Some of the best deals for organized bicycle weekends are offered through the local cycling clubs. The Potomac Pedalers (see Bike Organizations) runs weekend events in the spring to Lewes, Delaware, and summer weekends in the Shenandoah Valley. Their largest event, the Fall Frolic, is held near Hagerstown, Maryland. The Baltimore Bicycle Club (410–792–8308) also offers excellent weekend events, including the Spring Fling at Chestertown, Maryland. You don't have to be a member of these organizations to sign up.

Spokes, a free newspaper distributed in most bike shops, lists bicycling events within several hundred miles of Washington, including commercial rides, club events, fund-raisers, and races. You don't have to race; spectators are welcome.

About the Authors

Michael Leccese has been a bike commuter, tourist, and occasional racer for 30 years. He has written for the *New York Times*, the *Washington Post*, and *USA Today*, and with his wife, Kathleen McCormick, written or edited several books on architecture and planning. The New York native now lives in Boulder, Colorado, where he is principal of Fountainhead Communications. He is also the author of *Short Bike Rides in Colorado* (Globe Pequot, 1995).

Michael Leccese

Rolf Pemberton is a cyclist and outdoor enthusiast. His articles have appeared in *Ski Canada* magazine, and in both local and national publications. An advocate of riding etiquette and environmental respect, he founded and oversees a cycling club with chapters in Costa Rica, Canada, and the United States. He has cycled all over the world, has been known to race, rides in twenty-four-hour events, and continues to host annual "epic" rides about nothing more than the essence of cycling. Rolf and his wife, Kathryn, live in the D.C. area with dogs, a cat, and a whole horde of bikes.

Rolf Pemberton

worship:

wedding
to marriage